KV-578-909

Please renew/return items by last date
shown. Please call the number below:

Renewals and enquiries: 0300 123 4049

Textphone for hearing or
speech impaired users: 0300 123 4041

www.hertsdirect.org/librarycatalogue
L32

Hertfordshire

The Basque Region

WORLD BIBLIOGRAPHICAL SERIES

General Editors:
Robert G. Neville (Executive Editor)
John J. Horton

Robert A. Myers   Hans H. Wellisch
Ian Wallace   Ralph Lee Woodward, Jr.

John J. Horton is Deputy Librarian of the University of Bradford and was formerly Chairman of its Academic Board of Studies in Social Sciences. He has maintained a longstanding interest in the discipline of area studies and its associated bibliographical problems, with special reference to European Studies. In particular he has published in the field of Icelandic and of Yugoslav studies, including the two relevant volumes in the World Bibliographical Series.

Robert A. Myers is Associate Professor of Anthropology in the Division of Social Sciences and Director of Study Abroad Programs at Alfred University, Alfred, New York. He has studied post-colonial island nations of the Caribbean and has spent two years in Nigeria on a Fulbright Lectureship. His interests include international public health, historical anthropology and developing societies. In addition to *Amerindians of the Lesser Antilles: a bibliography* (1981), *A Resource Guide to Dominica, 1493-1986* (1987) and numerous articles, he has compiled the World Bibliographical Series volumes on *Dominica* (1987), *Nigeria* (1989) and *Ghana* (1991).

Ian Wallace is Professor of German at the University of Bath. A graduate of Oxford in French and German, he also studied in Tübingen, Heidelberg and Lausanne before taking teaching posts at universities in the USA, Scotland and England. He specializes in contemporary German affairs, especially literature and culture, on which he has published numerous articles and books. In 1979 he founded the journal *GDR Monitor*, which he continues to edit under its new title *German Monitor*.

Hans H. Wellisch is Professor emeritus at the College of Library and Information Services, University of Maryland. He was President of the American Society of Indexers and was a member of the International Federation for Documentation. He is the author of numerous articles and several books on indexing and abstracting, and has published *The Conversion of Scripts and Indexing and Abstracting: an International Bibliography*, and *Indexing from A to Z*. He also contributes frequently to *Journal of the American Society for Information Science*, *The Indexer* and other professional journals.

Ralph Lee Woodward, Jr. is Professor of History at Tulane University, New Orleans. He is the author of *Central America, a Nation Divided*, 2nd ed. (1985), as well as several monographs and more than seventy scholarly articles on modern Latin America. He has also compiled volumes in the World Bibliographical Series on *Belize* (1980), *El Salvador* (1988), *Guatemala* (Rev. Ed.) (1992) and *Nicaragua* (Rev. Ed.) (1994). Dr. Woodward edited the Central American section of the *Research Guide to Central America and the Caribbean* (1985) and is currently associate editor of Scribner's *Encyclopedia of Latin American History*.

VOLUME 212

The Basque Region

Geoffrey West

Compiler

CLIO PRESS
OXFORD, ENGLAND · SANTA BARBARA, CALIFORNIA
DENVER, COLORADO

© Copyright 1998 by ABC-CLIO Ltd.

All rights reserved. No part of this publication may be reproduced, stored in any retrieval system, or transmitted in any form or by any means, electronic, mechanical, photocopying or otherwise, without the prior permission in writing of the publishers.

British Library Cataloguing in Publication Data

West, Geoffrey, 1950-
The Basque Region – (World bibliographical series; v. 212)
1. Pais Vasco (Spain) – Bibliography
I. Title
016.9′466

ISBN 1–85109–258–7

ABC-CLIO Ltd.,
Old Clarendon Ironworks,
35A Great Clarendon Street,
Oxford OX2 6AT, England.

———

ABC-CLIO Inc.,
130 Cremona Drive,
Santa Barbara,
CA 93117, USA.

Designed by Bernard Crossland.
Typeset by Columns Design Ltd., Reading, England.
Printed in Great Britain by print in black, Midsomer Norton.

THE WORLD BIBLIOGRAPHICAL SERIES

This series, which is principally designed for the English speaker, will eventually cover every country (and some of the world's principal regions and cities), each in a separate volume comprising annotated entries on works dealing with its history, geography, economy and politics; and with its people, their culture, customs, religion and social organization. Attention will also be paid to current living conditions – housing, education, newspapers, clothing, etc. – that are all too often ignored in standard bibliographies; and to those particular aspects relevant to individual countries. Each volume seeks to achieve, by use of careful selectivity and critical assessment of the literature, an expression of the country and an appreciation of its nature and national aspirations, to guide the reader towards an understanding of its importance. The keynote of the series is to provide, in a uniform format, an interpretation of each country that will express its culture, its place in the world, and the qualities and background that make it unique. The views expressed in individual volumes, however, are not necessarily those of the publisher.

VOLUMES IN THE SERIES

Manterola
Liburudendako
lagunei

(To my friends
at the
Librería Manterola, Donostia)

Contents

Contents

Contents

Introduction

The Basque Region occupies an area of approximately 20,664 square kilometres on either side of the border between France and Spain at the western end of the Pyrenees. The Basque people have a strong sense of national identity and their own language, *euskera*. They speak of the Basque Region in historical terms as *Euskal Herria* (literally, both the Basque Country and the Basque people) and as a political entity as *Euskadi*. Indeed, the extent of Euskal Herria equates approximately with the area where there are still Basque speakers and for the nationalist it is also the territory which would constitute a nation independent of both France and Spain. It is made up of seven provinces, of which three are in France – Labourd (Lapurdi), Basse Navarre (Nafarroa Beherea) and Soule (Zuberoa) – and four are in Spain – Bizkaia, Gipuzkoa, Alava (Araba) and Navarra (Nafarroa). The population of the Basque Region is ca. 2,867,904. Of this figure 2,098,055 persons live in Alava, Bizkaia, and Gipuzkoa (Census 1996), 520,574 live in Navarra (Census 1996) and 250,161 live in the French Basque provinces (Census 1990). In the present-day political reality, *Euskadi* denotes the Basque Autonomous Community (Euskal Autonomi Elkartea), one of the seventeen regional autonomies of Spain.

The Basque nationalist movement has been, and still is, powerful, especially in Spain where it is represented politically by the conservative Partido Nacionalista Vasco (Basque Nationalist Party) and by the militant left-wing party, Herri Batasuna (Popular Unity). Since 1959, a breakaway group of the PNV, ETA (Euskadi Ta Askatasuna = Basque Country and Freedom), has waged a terrorist campaign in pursuit of political independence and unity for all seven Basque provinces. Regional autonomy is now an integral part of the Spanish Constitution of 1978, but the Spanish Basques still have no right of self-determination. Although Basque nationalists view Navarra as part of Euskal Herria, the province's position remains equivocal. During its history it has fiercely defended its autonomy, but as part of Spain rather than as an independent entity, and during the Civil War it was broadly on the side of Franco. In the 1979 referendum Navarra voted to remain an autonomous community separate from the other three Basque provinces.

Who are the Basques?

The Basques are an ancient people who have occupied their present territory since the beginning of recorded time and in fact the linguistic evidence of place-names and personal names suggests that they once inhabited a larger area, although its extent is a matter of dispute. DNA analysis and haematological evidence indicate that the Basques are indeed a people distinct from their immediate neighbours. This anthropological research has led some scholars to talk of a Basque presence in the western Pyrenees as far back as 10,000 years ago. However, although human habitation of the western Pyrenees dates from the Middle Palaeolithic period (c. 70000 BC), the archaeological evidence does not permit the identification of these settlements with a specifically Basque culture. The survival of the Basque language is further strong evidence of the Basques' antiquity and unity. Linguistically it is an isolate, unrelated to any surviving language and in all probability it was spoken in the Basque region before the arrival of Indo-European peoples (c. 2000 BC), the ancestors of today's French and Spanish speakers. Attempts to relate Basque to other languages or language groups, particularly Iberian, Caucasian and North African, have all proved inconclusive. On balance, therefore, the Basques would seem to have occupied their present territory since the Neolithic era (which began c. 4000 BC).

The land

The geography of the Basque Region comprises various contrasting features. The highest land is to the east of the Roncal valley of the Pyrenees, dividing Spanish Navarra from French Basse Navarre. From there the mountains descend gradually to the border between Navarra and Gipuzkoa. Another mountain range runs parallel to the coast towards the south of Bizkaia and Gipuzkoa and the north of Alava, forming part of the Cordillera Cantábrica. The coastal region of Gipuzkoa and Bizkaia is hilly as far as the sea, but is divided by longitudinal corridors. The French coastal region is by contrast flat and merges with the landscape of the Landes north of the river Adour. The central and eastern parts of Alava and Spanish Navarra are flat and form part of the Ebro river valley.

The Basque Region has two distinct types of climate. A relatively damp all-year round Atlantic climate prevails in Gipuzkoa, Bizkaia, northern Alava, north-western Navarra and the whole of the French Basque region, while a drier, Mediterranean climate occurs in southern Navarra and the south of Alava. The climate of the Pyrenees is sub-Alpine. The vegetation of the region corresponds directly to the climatic conditions, with broad-leaf woodland in the Atlantic-type climate, and smaller-leafed, spiny vegetation in the drier climate to the south. However, the demands of industry and commercial agriculture and forestry have altered and reduced the area of native vegetation. Pine trees have replaced indigenous trees in much of the Atlantic region.

Administration

In spite of the Basque people's strong sense of nationhood, the present-day Basque Region lacks political unity. Split between two countries, it is further divided by those countries' administrative systems. The Spanish provinces of Bizkaia, Gipuzkoa and Alava constitute the Comunidad Autónoma Vasca, or, de Euskadi (Basque Autonomous Community, or, Autonomous Community of Euskadi). Each province is further divided into municipalities. The establishment of the Basque Autonomous Community dates from 1979 when the Statute of Autonomy envisaged by the Spanish Constitution of 1978 was approved by referendum. The fourth Spanish province, Navarra voted not to join with the three other Basque Provinces, although the option remains open. In 1982, by a law known as the *Amejoramiento del Fuero Navarro* (Revision of the Navarrese charter), Navarra became an autonomous community in its own right, known officially as the Comunidad Foral de Navarra (Charter Community of Navarra). The three French Basque provinces, Labourd, Basse Navarre and Soule, together with Béarn, make up the department of Pyrénées Atlantiques. This latter in turn is part of the Aquitaine region with its capital in Bordeaux. The prefecture of Pyrénées Atlantiques is sited at Pau and there are two sub-prefectures: in Bayonne, covering Labourd and Basse Navarre, and in Oloron, covering Soule. The departments are subdivided into cantons and the latter into communes.

Each of the provinces of the Basque Autonomous Community has its own elected legislative body, the Juntas Generales (General Assembly), together with a corresponding administration, the Diputación Foral (Provincial Council). The Community in turn has a President (in Basque, *lehendakari*), Parliament (Parlamento Vasco) and administration (Gobierno Vasco). Both the Basque Parliament and Government are located in the city of Vitoria-Gasteiz (Alava). The Parliament has virtually sole responsibility for education, health, culture and housing and considerable autonomy in industrial and research policy, transport and communications. It also has tax-raising powers, enabling the financing of local bodies and services and the transfer of revenue to the central Spanish authorities for national expenditure. The Community also has its own police force, the *Ertzaintza*, and its own public radio and television (Eusko Irrati Telebista). Navarra too has its own parliament, the Parlamento Foral, together with its corresponding administration, the Diputación Foral de Navarra. Both bodies are located in Pamplona. The Navarrese parliament has tax-raising powers and responsibility for a similar range of services and activities as the Basque Autonomous Community.

The situation in the French region is very different. France is divided into twenty-two regions with responsibilities for local development and planning. There are direct elections to the regional councils, each of which is headed by a president. The French Basque region is subsumed into Aquitaine. However, since 1995 the Pays Basque has also had an elected council of sixty-five members comprising parliamentary deputies, regional councillors and representatives of mayors. Each department also has a directly elected General Council, headed by a president, with responsibility for local administration.

Economy

Industry

The present-day economies of the French and Spanish Basque regions are very different from each other, the result of more intensive and more rapid industrial development in the latter. There are also differences between the economies of the three Spanish Basque provinces and Navarra. The French region, which remains predominantly agricultural except for the coastal strip where tourism predominates, is poorer than the Spanish region. Industrial development is centred around Bayonne and in the industrial zones of Hendaye and Saint-Jean-de-Luz. The major activities are aeronautics, food industries, electronics and metal manufactures. By contrast the three provinces forming the Basque Autonomous Community, particularly Bizkaia and parts of Gipuzkoa, are considerably more industrialized. Heavy industries, notably iron and steel making and shipbuilding, were important for a long time in the Bilbao region, but these have declined considerably in recent years, leading to a high level of unemployment. Shipbuilding has since diversified and continues on a reduced scale, while the metal industries have specialized and produce high-quality products. New manufacturing industries, such as machine tools, aerospace and electronics, have developed and prospered. Gipuzkoa has a concentration of heavy industry around the port of Pasajes, particularly shipbuilding, steel processing and metal manufactures. Important steel companies are also located at Legazpia, Zumárraga and Bergara. Other important industries in the Basque Autonomous Community are chemicals, rubber manufactures, plastics, paper and textiles. A notable feature of the region's industry are the co-operatives, particularly those at Mondragón, which produce a wide range of products from foodstuffs to white goods and motor vehicles. The service sector has grown in importance, accounting for 59.5 per cent of employment in the Basque Autonomous Community in 1998 (Source: EUSTAT Population with relation to activity survey; website: http://www.eustat.es). The most important industries of Navarra are metal manufacturing and chemical and food production.

Agriculture and fishing

The agriculture of the Basque Region varies according to the type of climate. Cereal and dairy farming predominate in those areas subject to the Atlantic type (the French region, Gipuzkoa, Bizkaia, northern Navarra and northern Alava), while in areas where the Mediterranean climate prevails, wheat, vines and olives are cultivated. A wider range of cereals is grown in the intermediate areas. The upland regions are given over to sheep, pig and cattle rearing, particularly the former where transhumance is still practised and follows traditional routes, some of which are centuries old. In the Spanish region forestry is assuming greater importance, the result of a policy of reforestation by which pines have replaced the native broad-leaf varieties. Reforestation is also a feature at lower levels in Gipuzkoa and Bizkaia where it has taken over the pastures of many *caseríos* or small holdings. These latter have long been a feature of farming throughout the Atlantic zone, although they have had to adapt to remain profitable, switching to market gardening in order to supply the needs of the urban areas.

Fishing has been an important industry in the Basque Region since the late Middle Ages with ports stretching the length of the Spanish and French coastlines. Catches of coastal fishing consist of tuna, hake, sardine and shellfish. Deep-sea trawlers, based at Pasajes, Bermeo and Ondárroa, fish for tuna, cod and hake. This activity has suffered considerably in recent years from EC restrictions on the size of catches.

The Basque language today

Euskera, the language of the Basques, is fundamental to Basque distinctiveness, although it is spoken only by a minority of the inhabitants of the region. According to statistics for 1995-96, in the Basque Autonomous Community 77.7 per cent of those asked considered Spanish to be their first language, and the remainder considered themselves either bilingual or to have Basque as their native tongue. In Navarra 89.8 per cent considered Spanish to be their first language, while in the French region 68.5 per cent saw French as their first language. This last figure is deceptive, however, as Basque speakers predominate hugely among older people, while among young people under sixteen, the rate of decline in the use of Basque is increasing. Conversely, in the Basque Provinces it is increasing among the under-sixteens and similarly in Navarra, albeit more slowly (figures from *Encuesta sociolingüística de Euskal Herria 1996* [Vitoria-Gasteiz, Spain: Gobierno Vasco, 1997].) Both Basque and Spanish are official languages in the Basque Autonomous Community. Spanish is an official language throughout Navarra, while Basque is also recognized as official in the Basque-speaking areas.

About the bibliography

The political and administrative divisions that fragment the present-day Basque Country, together with changes in the course of history, have not made the organization of a bibliography of the region straightforward. The traditional cultural and linguistic unity of the Basques allows the region to be viewed as a whole in some subjects, such as folklore, language and literature. At the same time the Basque Autonomous Community and Navarra now produce their own official publications, embracing promotional literature, statistics and a range of scholarly and specialist titles, which are applicable only to their jurisdictions. This is not the case for the French Pays Basque, which is lumped together in the Pyrénées Atlantiques and the even larger region of Aquitaine. It has been decided for the sake of simplicity to have just two sections within those chapters of this bibliography where a division is necessary, one for the French region and another for the Spanish region (including Navarra). The title of an item or the text of the annotations makes clear to which territory the particular work relates.

Place-names and spelling

The spelling of Basque place-names presents both a linguistic and political problem. The slight variations that exist between different forms of the same name in Basque (e.g. Nafarroa, Naparoa) could have been largely ignored. However, the great difference between Basque forms and the Spanish and French forms by which places are generally known to English speakers are so great (e.g. Iruñea = Pamplona) that to have used the Basque form would amount to excessive national political correctness. To refer to Bilbao as Bilbo would be as unnatural for present-day speakers of English as it would be to refer to Munich as München or Florence as Firenze. Thus, I have used the familiar French and Spanish forms, with two exceptions: Gipuzkoa rather than Guipúzcoa, and Bizkaia rather than Vizcaya. Not only are the places easily identified in their Basque forms, but these latter are now regularly used in official Spanish-language texts in those provinces. I have used Navarre, or Basse Navarre, to refer to the province in France and Navarra to the Foral Community in Spain. For the period when the two provinces formed a single kingdom in the Middle Ages, I have used Navarre. I have translated the Comunidad Autónoma Vasca (or, de Euskadi) as the Basque Autonomous Community. Euskadi, when it occurs, has not been translated and denotes only the Basque Autonomous Community. To refer to the seven provinces as a whole, I have generally adopted the term 'Basque Region', being the title of this book, and occasionally 'Basque Country', the name which in fact I would have preferred. I have rarely spoken of Euskadi in its broadest sense or of Euskal Herria, for the reason given already in this paragraph.

Acknowledgements

I am grateful to many people for their assistance and advice in the compilation and writing of this bibliography. In particular I should like to thank Carmen Gómez and Jesús Zubiaga who made me most welcome in the wonderful library of the Fundación Sancho el Sabio (Vitoria-Gasteiz) and who also answered a number of bibliographical queries; and Begoña Urigüen of the Servicio de Archivo y Documentación of the Basque Government in Vitoria-Gasteiz. At the outset of the project I benefitted from the resources of two libraries with which I was already familiar and I am grateful to Carmen Bilbao of Koldo Mitxelena Kulturunea, Donostia-San Sebastián, and to José Antonio Arana Martija and his staff at the library of Euskaltzaindia (Real Academia de la Lengua Vasca) in Bilbao. Throughout the compilation of the bibliography I have enjoyed the encouragement and warm hospitality of my friends at the Librería Manterola in Donostia-San Sebastián and also privileged access to their stock. The majority of the books cited herein, however, are to be found in the collection of the British Library, the range and depth of which never ceases to amaze even those employed here. I am grateful to my colleagues in Reader Services who speedily and efficiently retrieved so many books for me from the basements of our new building at St Pancras in the first months following its opening. I have benefitted also from the advice and, on occasions, the rescue service of my colleague, Alison Hill, in the word processing of the text and indexes. Dawn Olney gave me invaluable help with the preparation and correction of the indexes. Dr Roger Collins and Jesús Zubiaga read the introduction and made valuable suggestions for its improvement. Julia Goddard of ABC-CLIO Ltd has been a most patient and tolerant editor. None of those mentioned here are responsible for the bibliography's inevitable shortcomings and omissions.

I wish also to acknowledge the financial assistance provided by a grant from the British Academy which enabled me to consult in the library of the Basque Government official publications not available here in London. The British Library generously allowed me a period of study leave in the Basque Country which permitted me to take up the grant.

Geoffrey West
London
October 1998

Chronology

c. 77 BC	Pompey founds Roman settlement at Pamplona.
c. 7 AD	The Greek historian Strabo refers to a people settled in the western Pyrenees, the 'Vasconians' and to other obscure tribes: the 'Bardyetae' (possibly from Gipuzkoa); and the 'Allotriges' (possibly from Bizkaia).
c. 45	The Roman geographer Pomponius Mela refers to the 'Varduli' (from Gipuzkoa, probably equivalent to Strabo's 'Bardyetae').
c. 400	The Hispano-Roman poet Prudentius composes his *Peristephanon*, possibly on the occasion of the consecration of Calahorra cathedral (now Prov. Logroño), still in the land of the Vascones.
409	The Suevi, Alans and Vandals enter Spain through the western Pyrenees.
415	Visigoths invade Spain as allies of Rome.
late 5th century	Completion of diocesan structure in Spain. However, some Basques remained pagan until the 11th century.
late 6th century	Basques advance north of Pyrenees into Aquitaine.
711	Arab invasion of Spain. Limited penetration of Basque Region (occupation of Pamplona, 716-19, 734-40).
778	Battle of Roncesvalles: the Basques defeat the Frankish troops of Charlemagne.
c. 810-20	Iñigo Arista, the first Navarrese ruler, establishes dynasty in Pamplona.
9th century	Emergence of county of Labourd within duchy of Gascony. Emergence of Alava as county.
905	Sancho I Garcés becomes first King of Navarra.

1000-35	Sancho III Garcés of Navarra, the Great, rules León, Castile and Aragón, and has authority over French Basque region and Aquitaine.
11th century	Emergence of county of Soule within duchy of Gascony. Emergence of Bizkaia and Gipuzkoa as separate territories.
1134	King García Ramírez restores independence to Navarra from Aragón.
1152	Eleanor of Aquitaine brings Henry III Plantagenet Labourd as dowry.
c. 1180	The lordship (*señorío*) of Bizkaia and counties of Alava and Gipuzkoa recognize sovereignty of Castile.
1234	French dynasty of Téobald rules Franco–Spanish kingdom of Navarre.
1307	Soule recognizes sovereignty of King of England.
1449	Soule annexed by Béarn in Hundred Years War.
1512	Final division of Franco–Spanish kingdom of Navarre between Aragón and the house of Albret, Kings of French Navarre.
1545	First book in Basque printed in Bordeaux, Dechepare's *Linguae vasconum primitiae*.
1569-71	Second War of Religion in France. Henry of Bourbon becomes Henry III of Navarre (1572), subsequently Henry IV of France (1589).
1571	Leizarraga's Basque translation of the New Testament published in La Rochelle.
1610	Witchcraft trials in Labourd. Auto-da-fé in Logroño following trials of witches of Zugarramurdi.
1620	Edict of union joins Basse Navarre and Béarn to France.
1659	Present frontier established between France and Spain by the Treaty of the Pyrenees.
1789	The French Revolution.
1790	Creation of department of Basses-Pyrénées in France, incorporating Soule, Labourd, Basse Navarre and Béarn.
1794	French invasion of Spanish Basque region. Capture of Fuenterrabía and San Sebastián.
1795	Bilbao and Vitoria fall to French. Spanish territory eventually restored by Peace of Basel.
1813	Destruction of San Sebastián by English troops. Battle of Vitoria. End of Peninsular War.

1833-40	First Carlist War. Support for Carlism was strong in the Basque Provinces and Navarra where liberalism was seen as a threat to the *fueros*.
1835	Death of Carlist General Zumalacárregui at failed siege of Bilbao.
1841	Suppression of Basque *fueros*. Navarra ceases to be a kingdom and becomes a province but retains some economic autonomy.
1846-49	Second Carlist War.
1872-76	Third Carlist War.
1876	The surrender of the Carlists entailed the loss by the Basque Provinces and Navarra of the remaining privileges enshrined in the *fueros*.
1894	Sabino Arana (b. 1865) founds Basque nationalist organization, Euskaldun Batzokija ('Basque meeting-place').
1895	Euskaldun Batzokija folds but re-emerges as Partido Nacionalista Vasco (Basque Nationalist Party).
1919	Foundation of Euskaltzaindia (Real Academia de la Lengua Vasca).
1931	Proclamation of Second Republic in Spain.
1936	Outbreak of Spanish Civil War. Recognition by central government of autonomous Basque government consisting of Alava, Bizkaia and Gipuzkoa.
1937	Bombing of Gernika by German Condor Legion. Refugee children from Bilbao area evacuated abroad. Fall of autonomous Basque government; members of government go into exile.
1939	End of Spanish Civil War. Basque government in exile moves to Paris (until 1940).
1959	Formation of ETA (Euskadi ta Askatasuna = Basque Homeland and Liberty).
1963	Creation of Enbata in Pays Basque, committed to autonomy for the region.
1965	ETA conference approves use of revolutionary military tactics.
1968	Murder of a police inspector by ETA. Franco declares state of emergency.
1970	Sixteen ETA leaders put on trial in Burgos. Six receive a sentence of death, which is subsequently commuted. The department of Basses-Pyrénées becomes Pyrénées Atlantiques.

1973	ETA assassinates Admiral Carrero Blanco, President of the Spanish government.
1975	Execution of ETA militants under new anti-terrorist legislation.
	Death of General Franco.
1978	New Spanish Constitution successfully submitted to referendum; legal status granted to autonomies.
	Formation of militant nationalist party, Herri Batasuna.
1979	Alava, Bizkaia and Gipuzkoa approve the Statute of Autonomy, constituting the Comunidad Autónoma Vasca (Basque Autonomous Community). Navarra votes not to join.
1982	Navarra becomes separate autonomous community, the Comunidad Foral de Navarra ('Charter Community of Navarra').
1995	Setting up of regional council of French Basque Region.

The Region and Its People

General

1 **Aimery Picaud and the Basques: selections from** *The Pilgrim's Guide* **to Santiago de Compostela.**
Rachel Bard. *Essays in Basque social anthropology and history.* Edited by William A. Douglass. Reno, Nevada: Basque Studies Program, University of Nevada, 1989, p. 189-213. (Basque Studies Program Occasional Papers Series, no. 4).

A cleric from Poitou, Aimery Picaud is the probable author of a 12th-century Latin guide to the famous medieval pilgrimage, one of whose routes passed through the Pyrenean Basque region and Navarra. Aimery warns the pilgrim against the Basques, describing them in most unflattering terms as wicked, debauched, perverse, impious, violent, etc. Bard includes a number of key passages in English translation.

2 **The Basque country.**
Vivian Rowe. London: Putnam, 1955. 247p. map.

A description of the region and its inhabitants in the form of an imaginary journey from Bayonne to San Sebastián, via the French provinces, Pamplona, Vitoria and the coastal resorts. As well as the usual descriptions of dances, oral poets, the San Fermín festival and the game pelota, there are passages on the pilgrimage to Santiago de Compostela, the French epic poem, *La Chanson de Roland* and Wellington's crossing of the Adour in 1814.

3 **Les Basques.** (The Basques.)
Jacques Allières. Paris: Presses Universitaires de France, 1977. 128p. map. bibliog. (Que sais-je? 1668).

A concise introduction to the whole region, covering geography, prehistory and history to the end of the Spanish Civil War, language and literature, Basque society, customs and way of life, the last extending into the 1960s and 1970s, albeit somewhat sketchily. The 'Bibliographie sommaire' is indeed what it claims to be.

4   **The Basques.**
Roger Collins.   In: *A European geography*.   Edited by Tim Unwin.
London: Longman, 1988, p. 89-91.
A succinct summary of the human geography and society of the Basques, the theories concerning their origin and language, the rise of nationalism and the present political situation.

5   **The Basques and their country, dealing chiefly with the French provinces.**
P. S. Ormond.   London: Simpkin, Marshall, Hamilton, Kent & Co.,
1926. 2nd rev. ed. 148p. map. bibliog.
Ormond's patchwork introduction to the region includes: a historical outline; chapters on traditional customs and festivals (the *charivaris*, the *pastorales* of Soule); pelota; the fishing industry of St.-Jean-de-Luz and Ciboure; the *fors* (traditional rights) of the Basques; and three popular tales.

6   **A book of the Basques.**
Rodney Gallop.   London: MacMillan, 1934. 294p. maps. bibliog.
Reprinted, Reno, Nevada: University of Nevada Press, 1970; New York:
B. Blom, 1971.
Remarkable for its time and still eminently readable, this book overshadowed many of the travelogues and other guides devoted to the Basque region that preceded it. It offers a detailed introduction to the people, their customs and their culture. It is especially strong on folk music, popular spectacles and dance, but there are also chapters on the origin and the language of the Basques, vernacular architecture and beliefs. The author draws both on his own observations and study and on the work of reliable authorities. The French region commands greater attention than the Spanish. The University of Nevada reprint has new photographs, an introduction by William A. Douglass and a brief life of the author by his wife, Marjorie.

7   **Être basque.** (On being Basque.)
Directed by Jean Haritschelhar.   Toulouse, France: Privat, 1983. 492p.
maps. bibliog.
A collection of substantial and important essays on the Basque Region and the Basque people, all written by recognized authorities on their subject. Georges Viers writes on physical and human geography, including the industrial economy. The section on Basque society includes contributions on anthropology (Jesús Altuna), the Basque character (Pierre Lafitte and Pierre Charritton), a polemical piece on rural communities and urban development (Julio Caro Baroja), on law and government (Maïte Lafourcade), and on recent history and politics (Jean-Claude Larronde and Idoia Estornés Zubizarreta). The section on culture contains contributions on the Basque language (Luis Michelena), literature (Jean Haritschelhar), art and architecture (Juan San Martin and Michel Duvert), music (J. A. Arana Martija), dance (Gaizka Barandiarán and Jean Michel Guilcher) and native sports and games (Haritschelhar).

8   **Europe's first family: the Basques.**
Thomas J. Abercrombie. *National Geographic*, vol. 188, no. 5
(Nov. 1995), p. 78-97. map.
An optimistic piece of reportage on the contemporary state of the Basque Region.
Abercrombie concentrates on the Spanish region – its agriculture, fishing and heavy
industry, sport and culture, and landscape, reflecting both modern trends and tradi-
tions. The social and political problems of unemployment and terrorism are
underestimated.

9   **Euskal Herria, esentziak.** (The essence of the Basque Country.)
Photographs by Xabi Otero.   Arraoiz, Spain: Txoria Errekan, 1997.
111p. map.
Described as a 'visual overview of the heritage of the Basque Country', this work
consists of thirty-seven separate sections covering topics such as language, landscape,
furniture, architecture and folklore. The very brief texts, many by noted writers, are
printed in parallel in Basque, English, French and Spanish. The photographs are the
single most distinctive feature.

10   **El País Vasco.** (The Basque Country.)
Pío Baroja.   Barcelona: Ediciones Destino, 1953. 519p. 5 maps.
(Guías de España).
Pío Baroja, the novelist, who was himself Basque, spent a number of years as a country
doctor travelling on foot or on horseback through the Spanish Basque countryside. His
description of both the French and Spanish regions is very personal. He regrets change
and feels a greater affinity with the country than with the towns. Nonetheless, he
writes enthusiastically of the energy of industrial Bilbao. He does not like San
Sebastián, and sees its tourist influx as symptomatic of the lack of sociability and culture
of modern life. The final chapter is devoted to Basque popular poetry, music and
painting. The black-and-white photographs of Ramón Dimas are excellent.

11   **Pays Basques de France et d'Espagne.** (The Basque Country of France
and Spain.)
Rodney Gallop, Philippe Veyrin.   Paris; Grenoble, France: B. Arthaud,
1951. 32p. plates.
A collection of black-and-white photographs of people and places by Gallop, with
preliminary geographical descriptions by Veyrin. The majority of the photographs are
of the French region and Navarra.

12   **A time we knew. Images of yesterday in the Basque homeland.**
Photographs by William Albert Allard, text by Robert Laxalt.   Reno,
Nevada; Las Vegas: University of Nevada Press, 1990. 104p. (Basque
Series).
A nostalgic account in words and pictures of the life of Basque farmers and fishermen
during the late 1960s, focusing particularly on the French region and on San
Sebastián. The photographs provide the main interest.

The French Region

13   The Basque country.
Paintings by Romilly Fedden, descriptions by Katharine Fedden.
London: A. & C. Black, 1921. 196p. map. bibliog.
A very full introduction to the land and the people of the French Basque region. The author deals with the various theories of Basque origin then current, language and history. The descriptions of towns and villages are not especially personal, but they contain plenty of observed detail and evocations of historical events. The reproductions of the watercolours of Romilly Fedden are a most notable feature.

14   Les Basques de Labourd, de Soule et de Basse Navarre. Leur histoire et leurs traditions. (The Basques of Labourd, Soule and Basse Navarre. Their history and their traditions.)
Philippe Veyrin.   Bayonne, France: Arthaud, 1947. 350p. map. bibliog.
(Collection du Musée Basque).
An introductory study of the French region, which shows an awareness of the wider extent of the culture of the Basque people. The work is divided into three parts. The first considers the physical geography of the region and the indigenous way of life, the character of the people (including minorities such as the *cagots,* a pariah group descended from lepers) and the theories about their origin. The second consists of a history of the Pays Basque from Roman times to 1940. The third part is devoted to Basque traditions and customs: language and oral literature, religion, social and family life, popular sports, clothing and agricultural implements.

15   Biarritz, Pau and the Basque Country.
Armand Praviel.   London; Boston, Massachusetts: Medici Society, 1927. 172p. map. (The Picture Guides).
A description of the architecture, landscape, character and way of life in the French Basque region, illustrated by sepia-tint drawings and photographs. The survey of the coastal strip extends from the bathing resort of Biarritz into Spain, taking in Fuenterrabía and its fiesta in honour of the Virgin Mary, as far as San Sebastián. Chapter two is devoted to inland Labourd, Soule and Basse Navarre and has descriptions of pelota and the *pastorales* and masquerades of Soule. There is a brief section on Cambo and its famous resident Edmond Rostand, author of *Cyrano de Bergerac.* Non-Basque Béarn is the subject of the final chapter.

16   A book of the Pyrenees.
S. Baring-Gould.   London: Methuen, 1907. 303p. map.
Not a guidebook, but rather an introduction and a 'sketch of the History of the Country' for the prospective traveller. The author concentrates on the French region, but his survey extends as far as Bayonne and into Spain to Fuenterrabía and San Sebastián. This is a well-written and intelligent account, which is strong on history, and which contains some interesting contemporary photographs (see especially the view of the promenade of San Sebastián, facing p. 48).

17   **The French Pyrenees.**
      John Sturrock.   London; Boston, Massachusetts: Faber & Faber, 1988.
      229p. 3 maps.
Sturrock devotes p. 5-54 to the French Basque region, starting with the coastal region and then proceeding province by province. This is not a tourist guide with lists of hotels and restaurants, although the author does indicate the most sensible routes for reaching the important places and sights. The information is basically cultural and historical, with descriptions of landscapes, and towns, villages and their buildings.

18   **Gascony and the Pyrenees: England's first empire.**
      John East.   London: Johnson, 1970. 154p. 2 maps.
Although focusing on Gascony (ruled for some 300 years by the English crown during the Middle Ages) and including Béarn, East describes both the coastal strip and the Pyrenees of the French Basque region. He also mentions English contacts with the region, referring briefly to tourists visiting Biarritz, but in greater detail to Wellington's campaign in the Pyrenees during the Peninsular War.

19   **In a hundred graves. A Basque portrait.**
      Robert Laxalt.   Reno, Nevada: University of Nevada Press, 1972.
      146p. (The Basque Series).
A series of personal evocations of life and people in a French Basque village some time in the 1960s. Typical scenes described include netting doves, the slaughter of a pig and an auction of contraband horses.

20   **Le Pays Basque. Soule, Labourd, Basse Navarre.**
      E. Goyheneche.   Pau, France: Société Nouvelle d'Editions Régionales
      et de Diffusion, 1979. 671p. bibliog. maps.
A most useful and comprehensive introduction to the history and human geography of the region. The author covers history from prehistoric times, economic life and social institutions, literature and nationalism in Spain. Brief descriptions of individual towns and villages are also included. The numerous large black-and-white photographs look dated.

21   **Visages du Pays Basque.** (Images of the Pays Basque.)
      Paris: Horizons de France, 1946. 167p. 2 maps. (Collection
      'Provinciales').
A collection of four introductory essays to the region: on the land and its inhabitants (Gaëtan Bernoville); on local institutions and the administration of the Pays Basque (Michel Etcheverry); on art and architecture, including vernacular styles (Philippe Veyrin); and on popular literature, including songs, oral poetry and the *pastorales* of Soule (Jean Ithurriague). The text is accompanied by black-and-white photographs.

The Spanish Region

22   **The Basque Country.**
      J. R. Jump.   London: Harrap, 1976. 32p. map. (Discovering Spain).
A brief introduction to the Spanish Basque region for secondary school pupils, covering geography, Basque origins and language, nationalism, industry, agriculture and customs.

23   **The Basque Country. A social and economic guide.**
      Vitoria-Gasteiz, Spain: Servicio Central de Publicaciones del Gobierno Vasco, 1997. 2nd ed. 295p.
This official introduction in English to the Basque Autonomous Community consists of colour photographs, schematic maps, statistics and brief texts. In spite of its promotional purpose, it is a useful source of essential facts and figures on the human geography, government, culture, industry and socio-economic conditions of present-day Euskadi.

24   **Doing comparative social history: North-West England and the Basque Country from the 1830s to the 1930s. An inaugural lecture delivered at the University of Lancaster on 12 June 1996.**
      John K. Walton.   [Lancaster, England: University of Lancaster, 1996?]. 18p.
Contrasts the strong regional identity that exists in the Basque region of Spain in spite of differences (e.g. between the societies of San Sebastián and Bilbao and indeed within those cities), with the absence of regional identity in North-West England where identification tends to be more with either town or county.

25   **Euskalerria.** (The Basque Country.)
      Vitoria-Gasteiz, Spain: Eusko Jaurlaritza, Kultura eta Turismo Saila = Gobierno Vasco, Departamento de Cultura y Turismo, 1987. 206p.
Contains four brief, introductory essays in English on the history, language, art and architecture, and economy of the Basque region and of the three Basque Provinces in particular, and one on the image of the Basque in literature. They are all translated from Spanish and do not read particularly well. In fact, apart from the essay on the economy, useful for non-specialists, the photographs of Alberto Schommer are the most notable feature.

26   **País Vasco.** (The Basque Country.)
      Madrid: Fundación Juan March; Barcelona: Noguer, 1987. 396p. map. bibliog. (Tierras de España).
A work not dissimilar to item no. 25, in Spanish, but vastly superior to it. It contains broad surveys of the region's geography (by Manuel Ferrer Regales), history (by Luis Suárez Fernández), literature (by Luis Michelena and by Elías Amézaga) and visual art and architecture (by Salvador Andrés Ordax). It is well illustrated with black-and-white and colour photographs and has a fairly extensive bibliography.

Travellers' accounts

27 **Hill-towns of the Pyrenees.**
Amy Oakley, illustrations by Thornton Oakley.   New York: The
Century Co., 1923. 449p. map.
A rather wide-eyed account by an American of her three visits to the Pyrenees before,
during and after the First World War. Three chapters are concerned with the Basque
region: one each for the hinterland of the Pays Basque and for Gipuzkoa and
Pamplona, and one for the French coastal region. The illustrations are reasonably
attractive, but unremarkable.

28 **Navarre: the flea between two monkeys.**
Nina Epton.   London: Cassell & Co., 1957. 238p. map.
One of the best travel books on the region. The author recounts her travels through
both French and Spanish Navarre, with descriptions of fiestas, including San Fermín
in Pamplona, architecture (the monastery of Leyre, the buildings of Sangüesa and
Estella) and much historical background. Her narrative is further enlivened by her
observations about her fellow travellers and guests. The book's title comes from a
remark by Henri d'Albret, de-throned King of Navarre, referring to Navarre's position
between France and Spain.

29 **The romance of the Basque Country and the Pyrenees.**
Eleanor Elsner.   London: Herbert Jenkins Ltd., 1927. 319p. bibliog.
Combines an account of the author's journeys by car and public transport with the
usual speculations about the origin and language of the Basques. However, Elsner's
account is notable for her enthusiasm for much that she sees: the Musée Basque at
Bayonne, the coastline at Biarritz, and the Arenal of Bilbao, a city that she preferred
to 'fashionable' San Sebastián.

30 **The Spanish Pyrenees.**
Henry Myhill.   London: Faber & Faber, 1966. 272p. 8 maps. bibliog.
The author devotes some hundred pages to Navarra in his survey of the Spanish
Pyrenees from the Atlantic to the Mediterranean. He relates the history of the region
and describes its landscapes, people and fiestas, notably San Fermín at Pamplona. He
also provides plenty of practical information on roads and other means of transport.
The book is based on his own extensive travels and indeed his anecdotal recollections
of his own experiences and acquaintance with local people and Civil Guards add variety
to the account. He also refers to the writings of others (Richard Ford, Nina Epton, etc.)
who travelled in the region before him. Two other travellers have walked extensively
in the Pyrenees. J. M. Scott, *From sea to ocean. Walking along the Pyrenees* (London:
Geoffrey Bles, 1969), started on the Spanish side, but crossed into France soon after
reaching the Basque Region. Roger Higham's excellent *Road to the Pyrenees*
(London: J. M. Dent, 1971) describes a circular route from Orthez through Labourd,
Gipuzkoa and Navarra before returning to the French region and ending at Bayonne.

31   **Spanish raggle-taggle. Adventures with a fiddle in North Spain.**
      Walter Starkie.   London: John Murray, 1934. 481p. bibliog. map.

The author was an Irish Hispanist, academic and lecturer, and friend of gypsies, who journeyed across Spain one summer, paying his way as a wandering minstrel. His story is a mixture of traveller's anecdotes and the observations of the well-read foreign student of Spanish literature. He begins amid the bathers of Biarritz and continues into the Spanish Basque region, where he visits the painter Zuloaga at Zumaya, stops off at Loyola, before going to Ezkioga, then a place of pilgrimage on account of the visions (see item no. 178). He describes the sword dance at a fiesta at Villafranca de Oria (Gipuzkoa) before leaving the Basque region via Gernika and the train from Bilbao to Miranda de Ebro.

32   **Springtime in the Basque mountains.**
      Arthur Lazenby Liberty, with illustrations by Emma Louise Liberty and others.   London: Grant Richards, 1901. 299p.

An account of a journey through the French Basque region and into Spain undertaken by the Libertys, Arthur's sister and a female friend in 1897, based on Arthur's letters to his parents back home. These were subsequently augmented with maps and information drawn from published sources. They journeyed from Biarritz to Cambo, then on to Navarra as far as Pamplona. The fourth part finds them back at Cambo again. The narrative concentrates on their immediate experiences and frequent difficulties: grim lodgings, linguistic problems, waiting for meals and drinking rough wine. The amateur photographs were not a success.

Geography

General

33 **Bibliografía geográfica de Euskal Herria = Euskal Herriko geografia bibliografia.** (Bibliography of geography of the Basque Country.)
Edited by F. Javier Gómez Piñeiro. Donostia-San Sebastián, Spain: Instituto Geográfico Basco 'Andrés de Urdaneta', 1986. 459p.
A bibliography arranged under broad subject headings – physical geography, natural history, climate, geology, etc. – and then subdivided geographically into the Spanish Basque region, the three Provinces, Navarra, and the French Basque region. The majority of items are in Spanish or French, but some are in English.

34 **Bibliografía geográfica de Euskal herria: 1980-1992.** (Bibliography of geography of the Basque Country: 1980-92.)
F. Javier Gómez Piñeiro, Juan Antonio Sáez García, Marco Segurola Jiménez. San Sebastián, Spain: Instituto Geográfico Basco 'Andrés de Urdaneta', 1993. 306p.
A continuation of item no. 33.

35 **Geografía de Euskal Herria.** (Geography of the Basque Country.)
Francisco Javier Gómez Piñeiro. Barcelona: Oikos-Tau, 1985. 94p. maps. bibliog. (Opera Geographica Minora; Serie 4, Chorographia Iberica, no. 2).
A basic and very useful introduction to the physical and human geography of both the French and Spanish Basque regions, including Navarra. Gómez Piñeiro describes the physical environment, climate and vegetation, and then analyses population trends, industrial development and agricultural exploitation. Brief concluding sections cover

9

the local geography of the major urban centres and of the districts within each province. Inevitably some of the statistical data and economic information is now out of date.

36   **Itsasoa: el mar de Euskalerria: la naturaleza, el hombre y su historia.** (The sea: the Basque Country and the sea: nature, man and his history.)
Edited by Enrique Ayerbe.   Donostia, Spain: Etor, 1986-89. 7 vols.

An encyclopaedic work covering all aspects of the Basques' relationship with the sea from the earliest times to the present. There are extensive and scholarly articles on marine biology, climate, naval architecture, fishing, exploration and whaling, and the representation of the sea in art.

37   **The Western Pyrenees. Differential evolution of the French and Spanish borderland.**
Daniel Alexander Gómez-Ibáñez.   Oxford: Clarendon Press, 1975. 162p. 22 maps. bibliog.

This study of the relation between the international boundary (established in 1659) and economic and social associations of the valley communities embraces Navarra and the French Basque region. Gómez-Ibáñez compares and contrasts the landscape, climate and vegetation on either side of the border and demonstrates how valley communities were formed whose relationships crossed the political division. His chronological approach shows how such associations persist in spite of political and administrative changes and how the different rate and patterns of economic development in the two countries have impacted upon the Pyrenean region.

The French Region

38   **Pays Basque français et Barétous. Le relief des Pyrénées occidentales et de leur piémont.** (The French Basque Country and Barétous. The relief of the western Pyrenees and their piedmont.)
Georges Viers.   Toulouse, France: Privat, 1960. 604p. maps. bibliog.

A highly specialized and comprehensive geomorphological study of the French Basque region.

The Spanish Region

39   **Gailurrak eta goi lurrak.** (Summits and highlands.)
      Imanol Goikoetxea, photographs by Antxon Iturriza.   Donostia-San
      Sebastián, Spain: Gipuzkoako Foru Aldundia, Kultura eta Euskara
      Departamentua = Diputación Foral de Gipuzkoa, Departamento de
      Cultura y Euskara, 1995. 108p. map. bibliog. (Bertan, no. 9).
An attractively illustrated popular introduction to the mountains of Gipuzkoa. The text
– the English translation is appended – begins with a survey of the topography of
Gipuzkoa, followed by a brief description of its principal peaks, their physical
features, the traditions associated with them and possible climbs.

40   **Gipuzkoako karst eta leizezuloak.** (Karst and caverns of Gipuzkoa.)
      Carlos Galán, photographs by Francisco Etxeberria Gabilondo.
      Donostia-San Sebastián, Spain: Gipuzkoako Foru Aldundia, Kultura eta
      Tusimo Saila = Diputación Foral de Gipuzkoa, Departamento de Cultura
      y Turismo, 1994. 108p. bibliog. (Bertan, no. 6).
Looks at caves throughout the Basque region and their geology, before describing the
underground system of Gipuzkoa. It concludes with a brief history of speleology in
the province. The book is well illustrated and the English translation of the Basque
text is appended.

41   **Guía de minerales del País Vasco.** (Guide to the minerals of the
      Basque Country.)
      Gobierno Vasco, Departamento de Economía, Planificación y Medio
      Ambiente.   Vitoria-Gasteiz, Spain: Eusko Jaurlaritzen Argitalpen
      Zerbitzu Nagusia = Servicio Central de Publicaciones del Gobierno
      Vasco, 1991. 187p. map. bibliog.
A basic introduction to the minerals of the three Spanish Basque provinces, which
concentrates on twenty-four minerals at twenty sites. Each section includes enlarged
colour photographs and lists the properties and characteristics of the mineral, its uses
and where it occurs.

Maps

The French Region

42   **Hendaya, St. Jean-de-Luz: Côte d'argent.**
      Institut Géographique National.   Paris: Institut Géographique National,
      1995. Map size: 91 × 120 cm. Scale: 1:25,000 (1 cm. = 250m.).
An official physical map of the Pays Basque bordering on Spain. There are similar
maps for the Bayonne region and for the remainder of the Western Pyrenees.

11

43 **Pays Basque est.** (Eastern Pays Basque.)
Institut Géographique National.   Paris: Rando Éditions, 1982. Map
size: 89 × 120 cm. Scale: 1:50,000 (1 cm. = 500 m.). (Carte de
Randonées; Pyrénées Carte, no. 2).
A similar map to item no. 44, for the provinces of Soule and Basse Navarre.

44 **Pays Basque ouest. Labourd.** (Western Pays Basque.)
Institut Géographique National.   Paris: Rando Éditions, 1982. Map
size: 88 × 98 cm. Scale: 1:50,000 (1 cm. = 500 m.). (Carte de
Randonées; Pyrénées Carte, no. 1).
A physical tourist map indicating walking routes, ski resorts, etc. of the province of
Labourd.

45 **Pyrénées occidentales. Carte routière avec plans de ville & index.**
(Western Pyrenees. Road map with town plans and index.)
Institut Géographique National.   Paris: Institut Géographique National,
1998. Map size: 89 × 120 cm. Scale 1:250,000 (1 cm. = 2,500 m.).
A detailed road map which covers the entire region of the Western Pyrenees. The
individual town plans (there is one for Bayonne-Anglet-Biarritz) mark major access
roads only.

The Spanish Region

46 **Álava. Guipúzcoa. Vizcaya. Mapa provincial.** (Provincial map of
Alava, Gipuzkoa, Bizkaia.)
Instituto Geográfico Nacional.   Madrid: Centro Nacional de
Información Geográfica, [n.d.]. Map size: 74 × 98 cm. Scale: 1:200,000
(1 cm. = 2,000 m.).
An official physical map of the three Basque Provinces of Spain, with major roads and
railways and administrative boundaries clearly marked. Place-names are given in
Basque and Spanish.

47 **Navarra. Mapa provincial.** (Provincial map of Navarra.)
Instituto Geográfico Nacional.   Madrid: Centro Nacional de
Información Geográfica, [n.d.]. Map size: 99 × 98 cm. Scale: 1:200,000
(1 cm. = 2,000 m.).
A similar map to item no. 46, covering the province of Navarra.

Tourist Guides

General

48 **Discover the Basque Country. Labord. Lower Navarre. Soule. Navarre. Euzkadi.**
Camille Farnbon, translated by Simon Pleasance.   Vic-en-Bigorre, France: MSM, 1993. 191p. maps.
A guide to the whole Basque region, but concentrating on the Pays Basque and Navarra. It deals with the history and monuments of places worth visiting and on outstanding scenery, rather than on practical tourist information. The large colour photographs reach the standards expected today.

49 **Espacios naturales del País Vasco. Guía.** (Guide to the wild places of the Basque Country.)
Enea Itxina, Mikel Tellagorri.   Donostia, Spain: Elkarlanean, 1997. 28 maps. 323p.
A lavishly illustrated guide to the wildlife and landscape of the remoter parts of the Basque region.

50 **Le guide du Pays Basque.** (Guide to the Pays Basque.)
Manex Goyhenetche.   Lyon, France: La Manufacture, 1995. 3rd ed. 228p. maps. bibliog. (Les Guides de la Manufacture).
A tourist guide by a local historian in the form of eight journeys, predominantly dealing with the French Basque region and Navarra, but also taking in the Spanish coast as far west as San Sebastián. The introduction covers geography, Basque society, history, language and folklore. Subsequent chapters concentrate on buildings, local customs and festivals, and outstanding landscape. There are walking guides to towns and villages, plus lists of hotels and restaurants.

13

51 **Landscapes of the Pyrenees: a countryside guide.**
Paul Jenner, Christine Smith. London: Sunflower Books, 1997.
2nd ed. 136p. maps.

Includes details of two car tours, one in the French and the other in the Spanish region of the Basque Country, as well as seven walks in the mountains. The information provided is brief and practical.

52 **The Pyrenees.**
H. Belloc. London: Methuen, 1909. 340p. 22 maps.

Belloc's often quoted guide to the Pyrenees concentrates on their physical geography, although the second chapter does deal with the history of the region to the end of the Middle Ages. However, he devotes just fourteen pages to the Basque valleys in which he pays due attention to providing local information for the traveller, whether on foot or using public transport.

53 **The Pyrenees; the rough guide.**
Revised edition by Marc Dubin, original edition by Paul Jenner,
Christine Smith. London: Rough Guides, 1994. 479p. maps. (The
Rough Guide).

Chapter 5 is devoted to the Western Pyrenees and covers the French Basque region, Navarra and Gipuzkoa as far west as San Sebastián (p. 364-433). As with all guides in this series, it provides practical information for walkers and independent travellers on public transport, hotels and restaurants, together with an outline of historical and contemporary cultural information.

54 **Your guide to the Basque Country of Spain and France.**
Guy Sneath. London: Alvin Redman, 1966. 270p. map.

Although much of its information is out of date, this guidebook provides an evocative description of the region as it was during the 1960s. Its historical information is still valid. Charles Moore's *Free spirits of the Pyrenees. A guide to the Basque Country* (London: John Gifford, 1971), although readable, is superficial, particularly on the history, language and distinctiveness of the Basques.

The French Region

55 **Pays Basque. Béarn.**
Pierre Minvielle. Paris: Nathan, 1985. 256p. maps. bibliog. (Guides
Couleurs Delpal).

A comprehensive guide to the department of Pyrénées Atlantiques, vividly illustrated with colour photographs. The main text consists of information on places of interest, arranged alphabetically, and is preceded by a brief but wide-ranging introduction to the region and biographies of notable French Basques. Practical information (addresses of tourist offices, sporting facilities, and camping sites; dates of local festivals; brief lists of hotels and restaurants) is also included.

56   **Pays Basque: France.**
Paris: Editions Nouveaux Loisirs, 1994. 324p. maps. (Guides Gallimard).

An introduction to the French Basque region, densely packed with information and illustrations. There are introductory chapters on history, covering language, the pilgrim route and emigration to America; nature, covering climate, flora and fauna; art and culture, covering folklore, pelota, music and food; and architecture. The main section is organized by region and includes basic tourist information.

57   **South West France. Aquitaine: Dordogne to the Pyrenees.**
Francis Woodman.   London: A. & C. Black; New York: W. W. Norton, 1994. 191p. 11 maps. bibliog. (The Blue Guides).

There is no specific section on the Pays Basque, but p. 151-61 cover the area between Bayonne and Pau. As with other volumes in this well-known series, this guide is excellent on history, architecture, and museums and their holdings, but it does not highlight the region's Basque culture. The village of Ainhoa receives special mention, but St.-Jean-Pied-de-Port receives short shrift. The guide is intended primarily for visitors with cars and has little information on public transport.

The Spanish Region

58   **Alava.**
Micaela Josefa Portilla.   León, Spain: Editorial Everest, 1968. 157p. 2 maps. (Everest Tourist Guides).

Concentrates on the architecture of the historical buildings, particularly the churches, in the city of Vitoria and the surrounding province (e.g. the sanctuary at Estíbaliz). However, as with its companion volumes (items nos. 60, 62, 66), the detailed practical information is now largely of historical interest only.

59   **The Basque country.**
Ignacio Aldecoa.   Barcelona, Spain: Noguer, 1963. 61p. map. ('Andar y ver' Guides to Spain).

This guide, by a renowned novelist, offers an introduction to the land and people in the form of tourist itineraries. It is especially strong on architecture, but also includes short paragraphs on folklore, festivals and food. The supplementary tourist information is (inevitably) out-of-date, but the many black-and-white photographs retain their interest and appeal. Here the Basque country relates only to the three Basque Provinces; Navarra is omitted.

60 Biscay.
Francisco Sesmero Pérez. León, Spain: Editorial Everest, 1970.
158p. 2 maps. (Everest Tourist Guides).
The photographs contained in Sesmero Pérez's guide offer a nostalgic view of Bilbao, now much cleaned and modernized. However, the description and histories of the surrounding towns and villages are still of interest. Unfortunately the translation is dire.

61 Historic and monumental guide of Gipuzkoa.
San Sebastián, Spain: Diputación Foral de Gipuzkoa = Autonomous Council of Gipuzkoa, [1993]. 385p. maps.
A most detailed guide to buildings of historical and architectural interest in the province of Gipuzkoa, organized by municipality. Some 3,000 entries appear in the index to the extensive cartographic section (42 folded pages) and to the 65 rather small town plans. However, not all of the 3,000 items receive more than a passing mention in the illustrated descriptive section. This latter concentrates on outstanding buildings and includes a brief history of each municipality and information concerning its size, demographics and local festivities. Toponyms are given in their Basque form (e.g. Donostia, Deba).

62 Navarra.
Jaime del Burgo. León, Spain: Editorial Everest, 1966. 142p. 2 maps. (Everest Tourist Guides).
Del Burgo's guide to the province of Navarra, which includes sections on education, rail and road communications and welfare, is even more dated than its companions (items nos. 58, 60, 66). Included are sections on architecture and the usual sports and games (including speleology). The translation reads appallingly.

63 Northern Spain.
Dana Facaros, Michael Pauls. London: Cadogan Books, 1996.
Reprinted, 1997, 1998. 344p. maps. (Cadogan Guides).
A thoroughly excellent guidebook, which combines cultural information with basic details of transport, accommodation and places to eat. Two practical introductory chapters and one on history are geared to the whole of Spain, but appropriate and necessary references are made to the various northern regions. There are separate chapters on Navarra and La Rioja (p. 67-116) and Euskadi (p. 117-60). They include short sections on history, succinct descriptions of the major cities and towns of interest and references to significant buildings, museums and festivals. The authors' ironic sense of humour is a welcome addition.

64 Northern Spain with the Balearic Islands.
Edited by L. Russell Muirhead, 2nd ed. revised by John H. Harvey.
London: Ernest Benn, 1958. 457p. 47 maps. bibliog. (The Blue Guides).
Some thirty-eight pages of this guide are devoted to the Spanish Basque region and Navarra, compared with just over half that number in the 1993 guide, which covers the whole of Spain. Much of the original text concerning history and the physical geography of towns has been retained in the latter guide, but the practical tourist infor-

mation, which goes out of date so quickly, has been omitted. The modern guide is more suited to background reading and forward planning than to getting about on a day-to-day basis. The earlier volume has a section on the origins of the Basques, the modern one a section on the present political climate.

65   San Sebastián and the Basque Country. A companion-guide.
Trevor C. Smith.   Liverpool, England: Institute of Hispanic Studies, 1935. 94p. map. bibliog.

A brief introduction to the Basque Region, concentrating on the Spanish region, intended as a narrative guide for the visitor. A short chapter on the Basques and the geography of the area is followed by an itinerary which starts at San Sebastián and takes in St.-Jean-de-Luz and Biarritz, the Spanish coast as far as Bilbao, Azpeitia and Loyola, Oñate, Pamplona, Roncesvalles and St.-Jean-Pied-de-Port.

66   San Sebastián and Guipúzcoa.
José María Donosty.   León, Spain: Editorial Everest, 1969. 181p. 2 maps. (Everest Tourist Guides).

Of the Everest guides to the Spanish Basque region, this one retains the greatest interest, perhaps because San Sebastián has changed less than other cities in the region. Donosty concentrates on that town, its history, architecture and atmosphere, and on the neighbouring coastal resorts and harbours. There are paragraphs too on the male gastronomical societies, folklore and Basque sports. The numerous black-and-white photographs are particularly excellent.

67   Through the Spanish Pyrenees. GR11: a long distance footpath 'La Senda'.
Paul Lucia.   Milnthorpe, England: Cicerone Press, 1996. 224p. maps.

A practical guide for experienced walkers. 'La Senda' (the path), a high-level mountain trail, follows the Pyrenees from coast to coast on the Spanish side. It starts at Vera de Bidasoa and crosses Navarra via Elizondo, Puerto de Urkiaga, Burguete, Roncesvalles and Isaba to Zuriza in Aragón.

Flora and Fauna

68 **Araba, Bizkaia eta Gipuzkoako landare katalogoa = Catálogo florístico de Alava, Vizcaya y Guipúzcoa.** (Catalogue of the plants of Alava, Bizkaia and Gipuzkoa.)
Carlos Aseginolaza Iparragirre [et al.]. Vitoria-Gasteiz, Spain: Eusko Jaurlaritza, Ingurugiro Sailordetza = Gobierno Vasco, Viceconsejería de Medio Ambiente, 1984. 1,149p. bibliog.

A comprehensive work of botany, arranged according to the order of the *Flora europaea*. Latin names are used, as in the *Flora*, but Spanish and Basque terms are also given. The description of each plant details habitat, geographical distribution and rarity.

69 **Fauna de Euskalherria.** (Fauna of the Basque Country.)
Miguel Ibánez [et al.]. San Sebastián, Spain: Kriselu, 1986. 189p. bibliog.

A general introduction to some one thousand birds, fish, insects and animals native to the Basque region. The index includes Latin, Spanish and Basque forms of names.

70 **Guía de los árboles y arbustos de Euskal Herria.** (Guide to the trees and bushes of the Basque Country.)
Iñaki Aizpuru, Pilar Catalán, Francisco Garin. Vitoria-Gasteiz, Spain: Eusko Jaurlaritzaren Argitalpen Zerbitzu Nagusia = Servicio Central de Publicaciones del Gobierno Vasco, 1990. 477p.

Includes both native and introduced species. The arrangement is by family, further divided into species, entered under their Latin name. Spanish, French and Basque names are also given and are included in the index. Descriptions include habitat, flowering periods and geographical distribution, both in and beyond the Basque region. The text is well illustrated with black-and-white drawings and colour photographs.

71 **Vegetación de la Comunidad Autónoma del País Vasco.** (Vegetation of the Autonomous Community of the Basque Country.)
Edited by Antón Aranburu Albizuri.   Vitoria-Gasteiz, Spain: Servicio Central de Publicaciones, Gobierno Vasco, 1988. 361p. bibliog.
Description of the flora of Alava, Bizkaia and Gipuzkoa, which are divided into geographical areas, defined by their vegetation, geology and climatic conditions. The impact of population growth and development on the environment is also noted. The descriptions are at the level of species, although there is no index by species, only a glossary linking Latin botanical names to popular names in Spanish and Basque.

Espacios naturales del País Vasco. Guía. (Guide to the wild places of the Basque Country.)
See item no. 49.

Origins and Prehistory

Origins

72 **The Basque population and ancient migrations in Europe.**
Luca L. Cavalli-Sforza. In: *Congreso de Antropología (II Congreso Mundial Vasco).* San Sebastián, Spain: Gobierno Vasco; Sociedad de Ciencias Aranzadi, 1988, p. 129-37. (*Munibe Antropología-Arqueología*: suplemento, no. 6).

The genetic make-up of the modern Basque population – a high incidence of Rh-negative genes – distinguishes them from their neighbours. This, allied to linguistic evidence, suggests that they may represent the most direct descendants of Cro-Magnon people. Although early Neolithic farmers, possibly Indo-European speaking, spread from the Middle East or Asia Minor into Europe, the Basque language remained relatively impervious to external linguistic influences, possibly, Cavalli-Sforza argues, because of the distinctive features of the Basque social structure.

73 **The ethnogenesis of the Basques.**
Roger Collins. In: *Typen der Ethnogenese unter besonderer Berücksichtigung der Bayern.* Part One, compiled by Herwig Wolfram, Walter Pohl. Vienna: Österreichische Akademie der Wissenschaften, 1990, p. 35-44. (Veröffentlichungen der Kommission für Frühmittelalterforschung, Bd. 12). Reprinted, in *Law, culture and regionalism in early medieval Spain*, Aldershot, England: Variorum, 1992, item VIII.

Considers the ethnic identity of the Basques in the second half of the first millennium AD. Indigenous written and archaeological evidence from this period is lacking and information is generally provided by non-Basque sources. From the late 6th to late 8th centuries, when the Basques owed no external political allegiance, Basque society lacked a central authority, was still founded upon the extended family, and showed a possible matriarchal inheritance pattern. Surplus manpower prompted emigration. Curiously, for so resilient a people, these emigrants were rapidly absorbed by majority cultures.

74   **The genetic history of the Iberian Peninsula; a simulation.**
Francesc Calafell, Jaume Bertranpetit. *Current Anthropology*, no. 34 (1993), p. 735-45.
A highly technical article which presents conclusions drawn from a computer simulation of the demographic history of the Iberian Peninsula, showing that the Basques have remained genetically differentiated, the result, the authors conclude, of cultural and linguistic factors, in addition to geographical remoteness and isolation.

75   **A genetic reconstruction of the history of the population of the Iberian Peninsula.**
J. Bertranpetit, L. L. Cavalli-Sforza. *Annals of Human Genetics*, no. 55 (1991), p. 51-67.
The authors present the genetic evidence for the differentiation of the Basques from the rest of the Peninsular population, a phenomenon that possibly dates from the Neolithic or Post-Neolithic age, but not later.

76   **The *Vaccaei*, the *Vaceti*, and the rise of *Vasconia*.**
Roger Collins. *Studia Historica*, no. 6 (1988), p. 211-23. Reprinted, in *Law, culture and regionalism in early medieval Spain*, Aldershot, England: Variorum, 1992, item XI.
Studies the mis-application to the Basques (*Vascones*) of the ethnic terms *Vaccaei* (who lived in the middle Duero valley) and *Vaceti* (a people whose real existence is unattested) by Latin writers of the 7th and 8th centuries. Collins also examines the labelling of all Aquitaine as Vasconia by some 8th-century writers, and not just the area corresponding to the duchy of Gascony.

The Basques.
See item no. 79.

Prehistory

77   **Iberia before the Iberians. The Stone Age prehistory of Cantabrian Spain.**
Lawrence Guy Straus.   Albuquerque, New Mexico: University of New Mexico Press, 1992. 336p. maps. bibliog.
The only available work of synthesis in English specifically on the prehistory of northern Spain. Cantabria here takes in the entire region extending from the province of Asturias as far east as Gipuzkoa, plus Alava. The work is divided chronologically by period and there is no specific section devoted to the Basque region. There is a chapter

on cave painting, which includes information on five sites in the region, notably Altxerri, Ekain and Santamamiñe.

78 **Pyrenean prehistory: a palaeoeconomic survey of the French sites.**
Paul G. Bahn.   Warminster, England: Aris & Phillips, 1983. 511p.
maps. bibliog.

A comprehensive overview of Pyrenean social and economic prehistory based on archaeological evidence. Chapter 3 is devoted to the Pyrénées Atlantiques and chapter 4 to the central region. Bahn examines the population's artifacts, their domestic animals, the available vegetation (there is scant data on crop cultivation), settlement sites and transhumant existence. Economic development is related to topography and to climatic and environmental change. The question of the ethnicity of the population of the regions is not raised.

The Basques.
See item no. 79.

History

General

79   The Basques.
Roger Collins.   Oxford: Basil Blackwell, 1986. 227p. 27 maps. bibliog.
(The Peoples of Europe).
Probably the only book in any language primarily devoted to the origins of the
Basques and to their early history until the late 12th century, by which time the fundamental surviving political divisions were established and the nature of their society
determined. Collins chronicles their often turbulent relationship with peoples on either
side of the western Pyrenees, which, while ensuring the preservation of their language
and culture, did not create a sense of nationhood. He is sceptical of wilder physiological
claims for their racial distinctiveness, and is scrupulous too in his use of the sparse
evidence for this most obscure historical period.

**80   The Basques in Aquitaine and Navarre: problems of frontier
government.**
Roger Collins.   In: *War and society in the Middle Ages. Essays in
Honour of J. O. Prestwich.*   Edited by J. Gillingham, J. C. Holt.
Cambridge, England: Boydell, 1984, p. 3-17. Reprinted, in *Law, culture
and regionalism in early medieval Spain*, Aldershot, England:
Variorum, 1992, item X.
Covers the history of the western Pyrenees during the second half of the first millennium
AD, when the region was a frontier zone between sucessive rulers in France (Visigoths;
Franks) and Spain (Visigoths; Arabs). Drawing upon Visigothic and Carolingian
sources, Collins charts the expansion of the Basques into Aquitaine, north of the
Pyrenees, during the second half of the 6th century, and the emergence in the 9th cen-
tury of the kingdom of Navarra, centred upon Pamplona, and its often turbulent
relationship with the Franks.

81 **A history of the Peninsular War. Vol. 7. August 1813 to April 14, 1814. The capture of St. Sebastian, Wellington's invasion of France, battles of the Nivelle, the Nive, Orthez and Toulouse.**
Sir Charles Oman. Oxford: Clarendon Press, 1930. Reprinted, London: Greenhill Books, 1997. 574p. maps.
Includes a highly detailed and exclusively military history of the final stages of the Peninsular War in the Basque Region. Events discussed include the destruction of San Sebastián, the surrender of Pamplona and Wellington's final crossing from Spain into France in 1813.

82 **The Jews of Navarre.**
Béatrice Leroy. Jerusalem: The Magnes Press, The Hebrew University, 1985. 278p. 3 maps. bibliog. (Hispania Judaica, no. 4).
A study of the Jewish communities of medieval Navarre, which were concentrated around Tudela, Estella, Sangüesa and along the frontier with Castile. Leroy describes the nature of the communities and the principal occupations of their members, which included moneylending and work as agents of the Crown. One chapter is devoted to the careers of successful Jews in Navarre and to their family histories. Finally the author looks at the position of the Jews as non-Christians and traces their history from a time of relative tolerance and peaceful coexistence (Navarre took in Jews from Castile and from France) to their eventual expulsion in 1498.

83 **The last Jews on Iberian soil. Navarrese Jewry 1479-1498.**
Benjamin R. Gampel. Berkeley, California; Los Angeles; Oxford: University of California Press, 1989. 226p. map. bibliog.
This study covers the turbulent period from the death of Juan II of Aragón and Navarra until the expulsion of the Jews from Navarre in 1498, six years after they were expelled from Castile and Aragón. Navarre came increasingly under the influence of the Catholic Monarchs at a time of internal tension. In the first part of his book, Gampel describes the everyday life of Navarrese Jewry, its communities, economic activities and social structure. The second half is concerned with religion and politics, the role of the Inquisition, the arrival of exiles from Castile and Aragón and the events leading up to expulsion.

84 **La Navarre au Moyen Age.** (Navarre in the Middle Ages.)
Béatrice Leroy. Paris: Albin Michel, 1984. 199p. 3 maps. bibliog. (L'Aventure Humaine).
A history of the kingdom of Navarre until its virtual demise at the end of the Middle Ages. The author concentrates on the social aspects of the kingdom, the nobility, clergy and non-Christian groups (Moors and Jews), before giving a brief chronological account of the confused events of the second half of the 15th century.

85   **Le Royaume de Navarre à la fin du Moyen Âge: gouvernement et société.** (The kingdom of Navarre towards the close of the Middle Ages: government and society.)
Béatrice Leroy.   Aldershot, England: Variorum; Brookfield, Vermont: Gower Publishing, 1990. 1 vol. unpaginated (Collected Studies, no. 335).

A valuable collection of eighteen previously published articles in French concerning the Franco-Hispanic kingdom of Navarre during its rule by French monarchs. The articles cover a wide range of subjects, including commerce, public building works and the situation of the Jews, as well as matters of state and government.

86   **With Wellington in the Pyrenees: being an account of the operations between the allied army and the French from July 25 to August 2, 1813.**
F. C. Beatson.   London: Max Goschen, 1914. 318p. 12 maps. Reprinted, London: Tom Donovan, 1993.

A detailed account of Wellington's progress through the Spanish Basque region following his defeat of the French at Vitoria in 1812. Beatson describes the operations at San Sebastián and, in particular, the blockade of Pamplona, the two battles at Sorauren and the subsequent French retreat across the frontier at Echalar.

Christianity and the Basques.
See item no. 174.

Diccionario histórico-político de Euskal Herria. (Historico-political dictionary of the Basque Country.)
See item no. 197.

Money, prices, and wages in Valencia, Aragon, and Navarre, 1351-1500.
See item no. 229.

The French Region

87   **1789 et les Basques. Histoire, langue et littérature.** (1789 and the Basques. History, language and literature.)
Talence, France: Presses Universitaires de Bordeaux, 1991. 255p.

The published proceedings of a conference held at Bayonne (30 June-1 July 1989). It contains twelve papers in French and in Spanish on the historical situation in the Pays Basque in 1789, the impact of the Revolution on linguistic variety and aspects of Basque literature at the end of the 18th century.

88   **Les Basques et leur histoire, mythes et réalités.** (The Basques and
their history, myths and realities.)
Jean Goyhenetche.   Donostia, Spain; Bayonne, France: Elkar, 1993.
353p. bibliog.

An analysis of the historiography of the French Basque region from the 16th-19th
centuries, and a sociological study of the historians themselves (class, background
etc.). The appendices are very useful: analytical tables covering historical themes,
number of books published and use of the Basque language; lists of archival and
manuscript resources; and bibliography.

89   **Bayonne et la région bayonnaise du XIIe au XVe siècle. Études
d'histoire économique et sociale.** (Bayonne and the Bayonne region
from the 12th to the 15th century. Studies in economic and social
history.)
E. Goyheneche.   Bilbao, Spain: Universidad del País Vasco, 1990.
541p. bibliog.

A comprehensive study of the economy of the Bayonne area during the Middle Ages,
covering agriculture, industry and external trade with Spain and Portugal, the rest of
France, England and Ireland. The study is preceded by a description of the physical
and human geography of the region.

90   **Bayonne et sa région.** (Bayonne and the Bayonne region.)
Fédération Historique du Sud-Ouest.   Bayonne, France: la Fédération
Historique du Sud-Ouest, 1983. 540p.

The published proceedings of a conference held in Bayonne (4-5 April 1981) on a wide
range of historical topics, including prehistory, architecture and ecclesiastical and commercial history of all periods relating to the Bayonne region. All the papers are in French.

91   **The decline of a Basque state in France: Basse Navarre, 1512-1789.**
Rachel Bard.   In: *Anglo-American contributions to Basque studies:
essays in honor of Jon Bilbao.*   Edited by William A. Douglass,
Richard W. Etulain, William H. Jacobson Jr.   Reno, Nevada: Desert
Research Institute, 1977, p. 83-92. (Desert Research Institute
Publications in the Social Sciences, no. 13).

A clear, chronological account of the separation of French Basse Navarre and Spanish
Navarra and the eventual incorporation of the former into France as a department in
1789. The impact of Calvinism and the religious wars in Basse Navarre are also dealt
with briefly.

92   **Historia de Iparralde desde los orígenes a nuestros días.** (History of
the French Basque Region from its origins to the present.)
Eukeni Goyhenetxe.   San Sebastián, Spain: Txertoa, 1985. 143p.
bibliog. maps. (Askatasun haizea, no. 71).

An outline of the history of the French Basque region from prehistoric times until the
1970s, preceded by a brief geographical description. The work focuses upon political
and economic history, with short paragraphs on culture and education.

93 **Response of the Pays Basque to the convocation of the Estates General in Pre-Revolutionary France.**
Helen J. Castelli. *Anglo-American contributions to Basque studies: essays in honor of Jon Bibao.* Edited by William A. Douglass, Richard W. Etulain, William H. Jacobsen Jr. Reno, Nevada: Desert Research Institute, 1977, p. 93-105. (Desert Research Institute Publications on the Social Sciences, no. 13).
Analyses in detail the complex reaction and response of Labourd, Soule and in particular of Navarre, which considered itself a separate kingdom, to Louis XVI's summons in 1788 of the Estates General (previously not convened since 1614) in order to solve France's financial crisis. Castelli adds a brief summary of the administrative changes that followed the Revolution, and which remain current, and of the events that ensued in the Pays Basque.

94 **The Revolution in provincial France. Aquitaine, 1789-1799.**
Alan Forrest. Oxford: Clarendon Press, 1996. 377p. 9 maps. bibliog.
Although dealing with the events of the French Revolution, its impact and aftermath in Aquitaine as a whole, Forrest devotes some space to the situation of the Basques. They were viewed with suspicion by the Jacobins because of their desire to assert their separate identity and preserve their own interests, and because of their links with their fellow Basques in Spain. During the Terror, in 1794, an attempt at mass deportation of Basques took place. Forrest also includes a brief account of French incursions into the Spanish region in 1794-95, which led to the capture of San Sebastián, Hernani and Tolosa.

Hills of conflict. Basque nationalism in France.
See item no. 201.

The Spanish Region

95 **The Basque children in England. An account of their life at North Stoneham Camp.**
Yvonne Cloud. London: Victor Gollancz, 1937. 61p.
Cloud's account of life in a refugee camp in England, as experienced by children from the Basque Country during the Spanish Civil War, is preceded by translations of letters to three Basque brothers at North Stoneham camp (near Eastleigh, Hampshire), and by Dr Richard Ellis's short account of his journey to Bilbao to examine the children before departure. Cloud herself tells of the difficulties experienced by the children and by those looking after them at the camp, and of the children's reaction to the news of the fall of Bilbao to the insurgents. (An educational video-pack, *The Basque children of Eastleigh*, has recently been produced by Hampshire Record Office's Archive Education Service. This pack recounts the children's journey from Bilbao to Stoneham and their life in the camp, using archive film footage and black-and-white photographs, supplemented by interviews and documentary footage supplied by BBC TV South.)

96   **The Basque Country and European peace. An analysis of German domination in Euzkadi.**
London: Autonomous Government of Euskadi, 1938. 34p.
An account of German penetration into the industry, trade and development of the Spanish Basque region, aimed at persuading Britain and France of the threat thus posed to European security. Particular emphasis is placed on the construction of airfields and artillery bases.

97   **The Basque phase of Spain's first Carlist War.**
John F. Coverdale.   Princeton, New Jersey: Princeton University Press, 1984. 332p. bibliog.
Begins with a lucid account of events leading up to the first Carlist War (1833-40) and of the conflicts between Liberals, Royalists and ultra-Royalists. Coverdale then gives a narrative account of the military conflict that took place predominantly in the Basque region until the failed siege of Bilbao and the death of General Tomás de Zumalacárregui in 1835. The opening chapter also attributes the strength of Carlism in the Basque region to a sense of separateness and to economic and religious factors.

98   **Bibliografía del siglo XIX. Guerras carlistas. Luchas políticas.**
(Bibliography of the 19th century. Carlist Wars. Political struggles.)
Jaime del Burgo.   Pamplona, Spain: Diputación Foral de Navarra, 1978. 2nd ed. 1,072p.
Includes both primary and secondary printed sources, including contemporary magazines and newspapers, arranged alphabetically by author or title. In addition there are sections within the alphabetical sequence devoted to persons (e.g. Fernando VII), periods (e.g. War of 1833-40) or broad subjects (e.g. ecclesiastical history). A brief commentary on each item is given. Documents in the Archivo de Navarra and the Ayuntamiento de Pamplona (Town Council of Pamplona) are also included.

99   **The British Legion in Spain during the First Carlist War 1832-1839.**
Compiled by Ronald G. Shelley.   Brighton, England: Spanish Philatelic Society, 1975[?]. 68p. map. (Spanish Philatelic Society Bookclub, no. 4).
An edited transcription of the letters of Charles William Thompson, who served with the volunteer Legion, which were the basis of his book *Twelve months in the British Legion*, published in 1836 (item no. 119). The brief introduction by Julio-César Santoyo reveals that the many British soldiers who died at Vitoria were deliberately poisoned by the local baker who supplied their bread. In spite of the interests of the publisher, the philatelic content of this publication is relatively minor.

100   **Carlism and crisis in Spain, 1931-1939.**
Martin Blinkhorn.   Cambridge, England: Cambridge University Press, 1975. 394p. map. bibliog.
In the context of a study of the ideology of Carlism in the 1930s and its relations with other right-wing political groupings, Blinkhorn explores the relationship between Carlists and the Basque Nationalist Party. Linked by their strong Catholicism and a desire for regional autonomy, an uneasy alliance was forged between them in 1931,

but this had foundered totally by 1933 on the Nationalists' increasing desire for full autonomy and sense of Basque nationhood. The author also examines the role of the Navarrese Carlists in the uprising of 1936 and the Civil War in Spain.

101 **Carlism – Basque or 'Spanish' traditionalism.**
Stanley G. Payne.   In: *Anglo-American contributions to Basque studies: essays in honor of Jon Bibao.*   Edited by William A. Douglass, Richard W. Etulain, William H. Jacobsen Jr.   Reno, Nevada: Desert Research Institute, 1977, p. 119-26. (Desert Research Institute Publications on the Social Sciences, no. 13).
Analyses the relationship between Carlism and Basque nationalism on the one hand and Spanish traditionalism on the other, the differences between them and attempts at alliance.

102 **The Carlist Wars in Spain.**
Edgar Holt.   London: Putnam, 1967. 303p. map. bibliog.
A useful account in English of all three conflicts (1833-40, 1872-76), preceded by a study of the dynastic dispute that prompted them. The significance of this conflict for the Basques, particularly in Navarra, is made clear: they saw in the Carlist cause the protection of their traditional rights (*fueros*). Holt devotes sufficient space to the British Legion, which fought in the First Carlist War on the side of the Spanish central government and the Queen Regent, María Cristina.

103 **The day Guernica died.**
Gordon Thomas, Max Morgan-Witts.   London: Hodder & Stoughton, 1975. 319p. map.
Gernika (Bizkaia), the traditional seat of Basque government, was destroyed by German bombing on 26 April 1937, in what was in part an experimental aerial assault on a civilian population. The authors' often moving narrative account is based on the personal testimonies of survivors and of German airmen. It amply documents the falsity of German claims that the Basques destroyed their own town. In the United States the book had the title *Guernica: the crucible of World War II.*

104 **Escape via Berlin. Eluding Franco in Hitler's Europe.**
José Antonio de Aguirre, introduction and annotations by Robert P. Clark.   Reno, Nevada; Las Vegas: University of Nevada Press, 1991. 391p. map. (The Basque Series).
José Antonio de Aguirre was President of the short-lived autonomous Basque government during the Spanish Civil War. His account of his experiences first appeared in Spanish in 1943 as *De Guernica a Nueva York*, then in 1945 in the United States as *Escape via Berlin* and in the United Kingdom as *Freedom was flesh and blood* (also 1945). Aguirre tells of events in the Civil War and of the fall of his government in 1937, of his exile in France and his subsequent escape from occupied Belgium in 1940. He became President of the Basque Government in exile, which met in New York in 1945.

105 **The fatal knot.**
John Lawrence Tone. Chapel Hill, North Carolina; London:
University of North Carolina, 1994. 239p. map. bibliog.

A study of the role of guerrillas in Navarra in the Peninsular War. Tone assesses the vital contribution that these forces made to the defeat of the French regular army which hugely outnumbered the combined armies of the British, Portuguese and Spanish. In Navarra, the guerrillas not only distracted the attention of the French army, but they effectively controlled the countryside, denying the French necessary tax revenues and the benefits of the rural economy. Tone attributes the Navarrese fighters' particular success to the nature of rural society in the region (rather than to their Basque-ness), and also to the leadership of Francisco Espoz y Mina.

106 **Foreign wings over the Basque Country.**
London: The Friends of Spain, 1937. 52p.

Contains excerpts from contemporary newpaper articles drawing upon eye-witness accounts of the German bombing of Gernika (26 April 1937). The publication was intended to dispel German and Nationalist propaganda that Basque Government troops were responsible for the destruction of the town.

107 **Great Britain and the blockade of Bilbao, April 1937.**
Michael Alpert. In: *Anglo-American contributions to Basque studies: essays in honor of Jon Bibao.* Edited by William A. Douglass, Richard W. Etulain, William H. Jacobsen Jr. Reno, Nevada: Desert Research Institute, 1977, p. 127-33. (Desert Research Institute Publications on the Social Sciences, no. 13).

A brief examination, based largely on Foreign Office records, of Great Britain's foreign policy during the naval blockade of Bilbao by Franco's forces. Alpert identifies the different attitudes of various parties at the time: of the Admiralty and elements of the Foreign Office (pro-Franco); of Foreign Secretary Eden (cautiously pro-Basque government); and of the opposition in Parliament and public opinion (pro-Basque government). He also describes events at sea and the breaking of the blockade by merchant ships.

108 **Guernica: being the official report of a Commission appointed by the Spanish National Government to investigate the causes of the destruction of Guernica on April 26-28, 1937.**
[Introduction by Arnold Wilson]. London: Eyre & Spottiswoode, 1938. 54p.

A report by the Spanish Nationalist side intended to counter the evidence and reports that Gernika had been bombed and burned by German aircraft. It consists of four parts: Wilson's introduction (he was a Member of Parliament and supporter of Franco); the report itself; a report of the inspection of the town; and the sworn evidence of witnesses. The sense of the report was to admit some of the evidence for the bombing, but also to harmonize it with the Nationalists' own claims that the Basques themselves had destroyed the town. However, the witnesses' testimonies at times contradict this interpretation and contain unexplained details that corroborate the original, and authentic, version of events.

109 **The Guernica generation. Basque refugee children of the Spanish Civil War.**
Dorothy Legarreta. Reno, Nevada: University of Nevada Press, 1984. 396p. bibliog. (The Basque Series).

As the Nationalist forces closed in on Bilbao in 1937, the Basque Government decided to evacuate the region's children to safety in other countries. Legarreta's account, often based on the personal experiences of the evacuees, tells of conditions in Bizkaia and Gipuzkoa during the Civil War, and then of the varied fortunes of the children in the receiving countries, which included the United Kingdom, France, Belgium, the Soviet Union and Mexico (the United States government refused). She also examines the various and changing attitudes of the governments of these countries to Franco's rebellion and subsequent régime and how these impacted upon the children's lives. There is a further chapter on the return of the children to Spain.

110 **Guernica! Guernica! A study of journalism, diplomacy, propaganda, and history.**
Herbert Rutledge Southworth. London; Berkeley, California; Los Angeles: University of California Press, 1977. 537p. bibliog.

The English version of Southworth's thesis, first published in French (Paris: Ruedo Ibérico, 1975). He studies the conflicting reports of the destruction of Gernika in 1937: the initial press dispatches from the Basque Country about the German bombardment, particularly those of George Steer (see item no. 110); the insurgent Nationalists' claims that the town was destroyed by the Basque army; and subsequent press reports along the same lines. The initial dispatches are vindicated and explanations are sought for the later press reports, together with reasons for the persistence of the controversy, particularly in France.

111 **Historia general de Navarra: desde los orígenes hasta nuestros días.** (General history of Navarra from its origins to modern times.)
Jaime del Burgo. Madrid: Rialp, 1992. 3 vols. bibliog.

A comprehensive, chronological history of Navarra from prehistory until 1850, preceded by sections on the historiography, geography, language, population and present-day political administration of Navarra. There is no analytical index, but the detailed table of contents facilitates consultation. The bibliography is extensive.

112 **The most striking events of a twelvemonth's campaign with Zumalacarregui, in Navarre and the Basque Provinces.**
C. F. Henningsen. London: John Murray, 1836. 2 vols.

Charles Frederick Henningsen served during the years 1834-35 with the Carlist forces whose cause he supported. After some preliminary reflections on the origins of the conflict and on the character of the Navarrese and the Basques, his memoirs focus very much upon the career and character of the charismatic general Zumalacárregui, who increased the size of the Carlist army several times over and moulded it into an effective fighting force, but whose death at the siege of Bilbao in 1835 dealt a severe blow to Carlist fortunes.

113 Navarra. The durable kingdom.
Rachel Bard.   Reno, Nevada: University of Nevada Press, 1982. 254p. map. bibliog. (The Basque Series).

A history of the Spanish kingdom, which was subsequently (1841) a province and latterly an autonomous community, from its beginnings until the early 1980s. The sections on the period of French rule (1234-1512), the Carlist Wars of the 19th century and the Spanish Civil War are valuable for illustrating the distinctiveness of Navarra from the three Basque Provinces.

114 Only for three months. The Basque children in exile.
Adrian Bell.   Norwich, England: Mousehold Press, 1996. 221p. bibliog.

An account of the experiences in England of the Basque refugee children, evacuated from Bilbao in 1937. Based largely on the refugees' own testimony, it tells of life first in the transit camp at North Stoneham, then in the various homes and centres ('colonies') to which they were dispersed. Bell also charts the shifting attitudes towards the Basque children of the British public and of politicians, some of whom, along with the hierarchy of the Catholic Church, were openly hostile. The focus then narrows, concentrating on those who were unable to return to Spain, on their experiences of work and of adoption. This fascinating book concludes with accounts of lives spent in England and of the difficulty and dangers of visiting Spain during the Franco era.

115 The Royal Navy & the siege of Bilbao.
James Cable.   Cambridge, England: Cambridge University Press, 1979. 219p. map. bibliog.

A full-length study of Britain's response to the Spanish Nationalist naval blockade of Bilbao during the Civil War. It is preceded by an account of the evolution of British foreign policy towards the conflict, and of intervention at sea in particular. The issues and events concerned the evacuation of Basque children and the use of warships to protect them. The author draws on primary material, including the messages from British representatives in Spain, the reports of naval officers and the records of ministerial and official discussions in London.

116 Ship of hope = Los niños vascos. (The Basque children.)
Oliver Marshall.   London: Ethnic Communities Oral History Project & North Kensington Archive at Notting Dale Urban Studies Centre, 1991. 24p. (North Kensingston Community History Series, no. 4; Hammersmith and Fulham Community History Series, no. 7).

A brief account of the evacuation of children to the United Kingdom from the autonomous Basque Republic in 1937, including the personal testimonies of three men who were not repatriated at the end of the Spanish Civil War. This is a bilingual edition in English and Spanish.

117 **Spain: the northern kingdoms and the Basques, 711-910.**
Roger Collins. In: *The new Cambridge medieval history.* vol. 2:
c. 700-*c.* 900. Edited by Rosamond McKitterick. Cambridge,
England: Cambridge University Press, 1995, p. 272-89.
On the basis of what little evidence has survived, Collins outlines (p. 284-89) the history
of the independent Basque kingdom of Pamplona, founded by Iñigo Arista in 824.

118 **The Tree of Gernika. A field study of modern war.**
G. L Steer. London: Hodder & Stoughton, 1938. 400p. 7 maps.
A detailed, first-hand account by the special correspondent of the London *Times*, concentrating on four phases of the Spanish Civil War in the Basque region: August-September 1936 on the Franco-Spanish frontier; January 1937 in Bilbao; April-June 1937 (General Mola's offensive against the Bilbao region); and August 1937, prior to the surrender of the Basque forces to the Italians and the former's betrayal to the insurgents. The third section includes information on the bombing of Gernika and is told in the greatest detail. Steer also deals at length with the British government's policy of non-intervention, and with Parliamentary reaction, particularly to the blockade of Bilbao by the Spanish Nationalists. Although limited in number, the contemporary black-and-white photographs tell their own awful story. Steer's pro-Basque account was subsequently challenged by supporters of the Spanish Nationalist cause, but in spite of occasional lapses and prejudices, his version of events, particularly of those in Gernika, has largely been vindicated.

119 **Twelve months in the British Legion.**
By an officer of the ninth regiment [Charles William Thompson].
London: John Macrone, 1836. 273p.
Thompson served as an officer with the volunteer Legion during the first Carlist War. He saw action at Hernani, Arlaban and at the victory at San Sebastián (1835-36). He sent letters back to his parents in England (see item no. 99), which formed the basis of his subsequently published account. In addition to relating his experiences in action and telling of the large numbers of British soldiers who died during the winter of 1835-36 at Vitoria, Thompson describes more mundane aspects of his time in the region, including visits to the theatre in Bilbao. He evidently believed in the cause in which he was engaged, as he describes the Carlist uprising as one of 'bigotry and priestcraft'.

120 **Vizcaya on the eve of Carlism. Politics and society, 1800-1833.**
Renato Barahona. Reno, Nevada; Las Vegas: University of Nevada
Press, 1989. 328p. bibliog. (The Basque Series).
Barahona's study of the background and origins of the First Carlist War in Bizkaia (1832-33) concentrates on socio-economic factors and class conflict. The upper classes, entrepreneurs, large landowners and some professionals supported liberalism and reform against the middle and lower classes, who sought protection in the provinces's privileges enshrined in the *fueros*. He also studies the tensions between the central government and the conservative *Diputación* of Bizkaia, determined to preserve its traditional institutions and socio-economic structures.

The Basques: their struggle for independence.
See item no. 196.

Basque nationalism.
See item no. 205.

Population and Migration

The French Region

121 **Un siècle de démographie dans les Pyrénées-Atlantiques.** (A century of demography in the Pyrénées-Atlantiques.)
Institut National de la Statistique et des Études Économiques.
Bordeaux, France: INSEE Aquitaine, 1994. 77p. maps. (Dossier no. 8, mai 1994).

Examines the increase in the population of the region, particularly on the Côte Basque, since the mid-1950s, which has been largely a result of immigration drawn by the tourist industry. This increase followed a gradual decline from 1846-1954 as a result of rural emigration. The statistical analysis provides figures for individual communes.

The Spanish Region

122 **1981eko Euskadiko Komunitate Autonomoko etxebizitza eta biztanleriaren zentsua = Censo de población y vivienda 1981 de la Comunidad Autónoma de Euskadi.** (Population and housing census of the Autonomous Community of Euskadi 1981.)
Gobierno Vasco, Dirección de Estadística. Vitoria-Gasteiz, Spain: Eusko Jaurlaritza = Gobierno Vasco, 1983-84. 7 vols.

The data, for the Basque Autonomous Community, was derived from the 1981 Spanish national census. The seven volumes are devoted to: population structure (analysis by age, sex, marital status, etc.); employment; education (including knowledge of Basque); population movement; birth statistics; family statistics; and housing statistics. The information is provided to a municipal level. There is a supplementary volume (xxi + 50p., 1985) covering seven new municipalities created between 1981 and 1984, with corresponding adjustments to the existing areas.

123 **Biztanleriaren berezko mugimendua = Movimiento natural de la población.** (Natural population changes.)
Instituto Vasco de Estadística. Vitoria-Gasteiz, Spain: EUSTAT, 1988. 210p.

A statistical publication which records the fluctuations in births (by sex, month, marital status of mother, still/live), marriages (by civil status, age and month) and deaths (by sex, civil status and month) for the Basque Autonomous Community, both as a whole and separately by province.

124 **Biztanleriaren eta etxebizitzen zentsuak 1991 = Censos de población y vivienda 1991.** (Population and housing censuses 1991.)
Instituto Vasco de Estadística. Vitoria-Gasteiz, Spain: EUSTAT, 1993. 6 vols.

The six volumes cover the population structure of the Basque Autonomous Community, employment, education and knowledge of Basque, population movement, family and birth statistics and housing.

125 **Censo de población 1991. Población de hecho. Por edades y sexos. Según zonas básicas.** (1991 Population census. Actual population. By age and sex. According to basic zones.)
Pamplona, Spain: Gobierno de Navarra, Departamento de Economía y Hacienda, Sección de Estadística, 1993. 1 vol. (no pagination). Printed recto only.

Population figures for Navarra are drawn from the 1991 national census. The analysis is solely by age and sex, according to area (*zona*) and community (*comunidad*).

126 **Euskadiko K.A.ko 1986ko biztanleen udal-errolda = Padrón municipal de habitantes 1986 de la C.A. de Euskadi.** (Municipal population census of the Autonomous Community of Euskadi 1986.)
Instituto Vasco de Estadística. Vitoria-Gasteiz, Spain: EUSTAT, 1988-89. 4 vols.

Provides the results of the 1986 census in the Basque Autonomous Community. The four volumes cover population structure, employment, population movement and education and knowledge of Basque. A supplement covers the nine municipalities created between 1 April 1986 and 3 July 1989.

127 **Serie demografiko homogenoak = Series demográficas homogenéas:
1970-1986.** (Homogeneous demographic series: 1970-86.)
Instituto Vasco de Estadística. Vitoria-Gasteiz, Spain: EUSTAT,
[1990]. 198p.

Includes unpublished material relating to the Basque Autonomous Community from
the national housing and population census of 1970 and the municipal census of 1975,
together with comparative tables from subsequent censuses (1981, 1986).

Migration

128 **Amerikanuak. Basques in the New World.**
William A. Douglass, Jon Bilbao. Reno, Nevada: University of
Nevada Press, 1975. 519p. 2 maps. bibliog. (The Basque Series).

The emigration of Basques from Europe began during the Age of Discovery, when
they left Spain for the New World as explorers, soldiers, settlers and missionaries. In
what is still the most significant book on Basque emigration and communities in the
Americas, Douglass and Bilbao chronicle the contribution of Basques to the Spanish
overseas empire, the continued exodus during the 19th century and their settlement in
both South America and the western states of the United States. They then examine
the emigrants' way of life and their maintenance of a distinctive Basque ethnicity. The
authors based their work on archival holdings in North and South America and, for
their study of the communities in Nevada and California, on interviews, in addition to
newspapers, biographies and government documents. The bibliography is substantial.

129 **Anglo-American contributions to Basque studies: essays in honor
of Jon Bilbao.**
Edited by William A. Douglass, Richard W. Etulain, William H.
Jacobsen, Jr. Reno, Nevada: Desert Research Institute, 1977. 221p.
(Desert Research Institute Publications on the Social Sciences, no. 13).

This collection of articles includes six devoted to Basques in the New World: Richard
W. Etulain, 'The Basques in Western North American literature' (p. 7-18); Joseph
Castelli, 'The Basque community in Buffalo, Wyoming' (p. 19-31); Richard H. Lane,
'Trouble in the sweet promised land: Basques in early twentieth century Northeastern
Nevada' (p. 33-41); Candi de Alaiza, 'Basque dancing in Southern California' (p. 43-50);
Frank P. Araujo, 'Basque ethnoveterinary practices in the San Joaquin Valley of
California' (p. 51-58); and Lorin R. Gaarder, 'Preliminary comments on the Basque
colony in Mexico City' (p. 59-69).

130 **La aventura vasca. Destino: Montevideo.** (The Basque adventure.
Destination: Montevideo.)
Martha Marenales Rossi. Montevideo: Gamacor Producciones,
Uruguay, 1991. 335p. bibliog.

A study of Basque emigration to Uruguay during the 19th century and its impact on
the economic and political life of that country. The first wave of migration began in

the 1820s and consisted largely of French Basques; Spanish Basques began to arrive in large numbers at the end of the First Carlist War (1840) and continued to do so until the end of the century. The author analyses the reasons for the choice of Uruguay as a destination: its liberal political climate; its need for skilled and unskilled labour in an expanding agricultural economy; high salaries in relation to cost of living; and success of the first migrants encouraging others to follow. Basque contributions included the introduction of viticulture and sheeprearing and a subsequent involvement in urban development. The last chapter examines the impact of persons of Basque origin on Uruguayan life in the 20th century. The documentary appendices include lists of migrants and of ships bound for Montevideo.

131   **Basques in the Western United States. A functional approach to determination of cultural presence in the geographic landscape.**
      Joseph Roy Castelli.   New York: Arno Press, 1980. 165p. 6 maps.
      bibliog. (American Ethnic Groups: the European Heritage).

A published doctoral thesis submitted to the University of Colorado in 1970. After a brief survey of European Basque culture which emphasizes those features relevant to settlements in the United States, Castelli considers the impact of Basque settlers in Buffalo, Wyoming, under the headings of social behaviour, education, politics and economics. Castelli records how Basque dances and celebrations have been retained for entertainment, but how at school Basques have taken up American sports, leading to the disappearance of the pelota court. In politics, Basques display an average American attitude focused primarily on protecting their own interests. The principal economic activity of the Basque Americans is sheepherding, although this was not actually introduced to the country by them. The home and the Church are seen as the two institutions responsible for maintaining Basque culture.

132   **L'émigration basco-béarnaise en Amérique.** (Basque-Béarnaise
      emigration to America.)
      Henry de Charnisay.   Biarritz, France: J. & D. Éditions, 1996. 270p.
      map. bibliog. (Collection Terres et Hommes du Sud).

A survey of transatlantic emigration, particularly to the River Plate region, from the Pays Basque and Béarn after 1825. The author reviews previous emigration from the region before analysing the particular causes of the large-scale emigration of the 19th century. He examines the problems of the agricultural economy, which the traditional Basque indivisible inheritance system only exacerbated, and the avoidance by Basques of military service, and assesses the attractions of a better life overseas, which were fostered by immigration agents from Argentina and Uruguay. The remaining chapters discuss the employment taken up by French Basques and Béarnais in the River Plate area, and the effects of the emigration in France. A general conclusion regrets both the loss of labour to France, and the migrants' gradual loss of contact with their French roots. The Pays Basque and Béarn were seen to benefit from the wealth that was either brought back by returning emigrants or sent back by those who remained abroad.

133 **L'émigration basque: histoire, économie, psychologie.** (Basque emigration: history, economy and psychology.)
Pierre Lhande. Paris: Nouvelle Librairie Nationale, 1910. 297p.

In a work considered by Jon Bilbao (item no. 402, p. 39) 'a classic in studies of Basque emigration', Lhande identifies its traditional causes: rejection of military service; the indivisibility of inheritance; and the activities of South American immigration agents. To these he added an 'inquiétude atavique' among the Basques – an innate restlessness manifest in a spirit of quest and exploration. He also examines the lives of Basque sailors, merchants, pirates and whalers in the North Atlantic and missionaries to Asia. The second part of the book is devoted to the life of the immigrants in America and to the effect of emigration in France.

134 **Essays in Basque social anthropology and history.**
Edited by William A. Douglass. Reno, Nevada: Basque Studies Program, 1989. 327p. (Basque Studies Program Occasional Papers Series, no. 4).

This collection of essays contains four on various aspects of Basque emigration: William A. Douglass, 'Factors in the formation of the New-World Basque emigrant diaspora' (p. 251-67), item no. 136; Kay Hummel, 'A wanted man: the Basque, el cojo Gómez, in Colombia' (p. 269-95); Jerónima Echeverría, 'California's Basque hotels and their *hoteleros*' (p. 297-316); and Gretchen Osa, 'The Overland: the last Basque hotel' (p. 317-23).

135 **An estimate of Navarrese migration in the second half of the nineteenth century (1879-1883).**
Angel García-Sanz Marcotegui, Alejandro Arizcun Cela. In: *Essays in Basque social anthropology and history.* Edited by William A. Douglass. Reno, Nevada: Basque Studies Program, University of Nevada, 1989, p. 235-49. (Basque Studies Program Occasional Papers Series, no. 4).

The relative stability of population levels in Navarra during the 19th century can be attributed to emigration, which counterbalanced population growth. People left for other parts of Spain and Latin America because of unemployment, disease and the effects of war. The authors present patterns of emigration by region and by destination, using statistics gathered by the Comisión de Reformas Sociales (Social Reforms Commission) in 1883.

136 **Factors in the formation of the New-World Basque emigrant diaspora.**
William A. Douglass. In: *Essays in Basque social anthropology and history.* Edited by William A. Douglass. Reno, Nevada: Basque Studies Program, University of Nevada, 1989, p. 235-49. (Basque Studies Program Occasional Papers Series, no. 4).

Essentially an overview of the approaches and topics covered in studies of migration: historical factors encouraging emigration from the Old World and factors inducing immigration to the New; chain migration (new migrants choose existing settlements); the impact of emigration on Old-World communities (loss of manpower; effect of investment of New-World money in the Old); and return migration, its effects and results.

137 **Historia de la emigración vasca a Argentina en el siglo XX.**
(History of Basque emigration to Argentina in the 20th century.)
José Manuel Azcona Pastor, Inés García-Albi Gil de Biedma, Fernando
Muru Ronda; Fernando García de Cortázar (editorial director).
Vitoria-Gasteiz, Spain: Eusko Jaurlaritzaren Argitalpen Zerbitzu
nagusia = Servicio Central de Publicaciones del Gobierno Vasco, 1992.
530p. bibliog. (Amerika eta Euskaldunak = America y los Vascos, 8).

This substantial study examines first the reasons for continued Basque emigration
from Spain to Argentina in the 20th century and the laws and regulations governing
immigration into that country. The third chapter looks at the practical details and
physical conditions of the transatlantic crossing, both in theory and reality. The
remaining chapters study the incorporation of Basques into the economic and social
life of Argentina, and the persistence of Basque culture, particularly following the
Spanish Civil War. An important feature of this book is the substantial appendix,
containing statistics of emigration and immigration, interviews with immigrants,
details of ships and shipping lines and reproductions of a variety of original
documents. The commemoration of 1492 prompted the publication of a number of
other works on Basques in the Americas, including Angel Mari Arrieta, *Emigración
alavesa a América en el siglo XIX* (Vitoria-Gasteiz, Spain: Gobierno Vasco, 1992) and
a substantial exhibition catalogue, *Presencia vasca en América* (Vitoria-Gasteiz,
Spain: Gobierno Vasco, 1991).

138 **Los paraísos posibles. Historia de la emigración vasca a Argentina
y Uruguay en el siglo XIX.** (Possible paradises. The history of Basque
emigration to Argentina and Uruguay in the 19th century.)
José Manuel Azcona Pastor. Bilbao, Spain: Universidad de Deusto,
1992. 333p. bibliog.

A historical study focusing on emigration from the Spanish Basque region to the River
Plate area. Azcona Pastor analyses the efforts of the Argentinian and Uruguayan
governments to encourage immigration, and the relevant laws and regulations, and
details the attractions (economic opportunities) for migrants. He also examines the
factors prompting emigration: the traditional indivisibility of inheritance in the Basque
Country; the lack of land for agricultural development; the disturbance and changes
produced by the Carlist Wars; and enforced military service. The role of agents, some
of whom were disreputable, working on behalf of South American companies, is also
examined, as is the reaction of the Basque authorities to the loss of labour. The latter
was generally limited to ensuring that the law was complied with. The final two
chapters look at the varying fortunes of Basque immigrants to Uruguay and Argentina
and the occupations that they took up.

139 **Vascos en Cuba, 1492-1511.** (Basques in Cuba, 1492-1511.)
Jon Bilbao. Buenos Aires: Editorial Vasca Ekin, 1958. 308p.
(Biblioteca de cultura vasca, no. 51).

Bilbao noted the relatively large number of Basques, particularly from Bizkaia, among
the crew on Christopher Columbus's voyages to the New World. In this detailed study

he examines their role as sailors, merchants and settlers during the first years of Spain's colonial period. He also suggests that Navidad, the first colony established by Columbus, could have failed because of dissensions between the non-Basque and Basque settlers, who at that time would have spoken Basque among themselves.

Serving girls and sheepherders: emigration and continuity in a Spanish Basque village.
See item no. 194.

The demise of agriculture in Fuenterrabia.
See item no. 261.

Unrewarding wealth. The commercialization and collapse of agriculture in a Spanish Basque town.
See item no. 264.

Basque Americans: a guide to information sources.
See item no. 402.

Language

General

140 **Ancient languages of the Hispanic Peninsula.**
James M. Anderson. Lanham, Maryland; New York; London:
University Press of America, 1988. 144p. bibliog.

A brief description of Basque grammar (p. 105-09) is followed by a summary of the unproven theories relating Basque to North African and Caucasian languages (p. 109-10). A more substantial chapter (p. 115-30) examines similarities between Basque and Iberian, but without demonstrating a conclusive relationship between them.

141 **The ancient languages of Spain and Portugal.**
Antonio Tovar. New York: S. F. Vanni, 1961. 138p. bibliog.

Tovar devotes a brief chapter (p. 127-38) to the prehistory of Basque, its status as an isolate, its grammar and its more recent history and literature.

142 **Anglo-American contributions to Basque studies: essays in honor of Jon Bilbao.**
Edited by William A. Douglass, Richard W. Etulain, William H.
Jacobsen, Jr. Reno, Nevada: Desert Research Institute, 1977. 221p.
(Desert Research Institute Publications on the Social Sciences, no. 13).

This homage volume includes six specialist studies on the Basque language: Jacobsen on the locative suffix (p. 163-68); Linda G. Gastañaga, 'Gapping Basque constituents' (p. 169-75); Terence H. Wilbur on the comparative construction (p. 177-80); John Bollenbacher on the Basque passive voice (p. 181-92); Jeffrey Heath on verbal morphology (p. 193-201); and Robert L. Trask, 'Historical syntax and Basque verbal morphology: two hypotheses' (p. 203-17).

143 **Apellidos vascos.** (Basque surnames.)
Luis Michelena. San Sebastián, Spain: Txertoa, 1989. 4th ed. 250p.
bibliog. (Askatasun haizea, no. 8).

First published in 1953, this remains the most accessible and reliable study of the etymology of Basque surnames, soundly based on Michelena's own work as a philologist and on that of his predecessors. It consists of 634 alphabetically arranged entries, each devoted to a stem or suffix, and each giving examples containing that basic semantic element. A single index of surnames guides the reader to the relevant entries that will explain a particular name. The introduction is useful, especially as it points out the fallacies of some of the previous works on this topic.

144 **Basque.**
René Lafon. In: *Current trends in linguistics*. vol. 9, *Linguistics in Western Europe*. Edited by Thomas A. Sebeok. The Hague; Paris: Mouton, 1972, p. 1,744-92.

Examines the tendencies of research into all aspects of the Basque language, highlighting those still most relevant. It thus constitutes a most valuable introduction to Basque grammar for the specialist and it is accompanied by a selective bibliography.

145 **Basque.**
Mario Saltarelli, with Miren Azkarate, David Farrell, Jon Ortiz de Urbina, Lourdes Oñederra. London; New York: Routledge, 1989. 311p. map. (Croom Helm Descriptive Grammars).

First published by Croom Helm in 1988, this grammar of Basque is conceived as one of a series that aims to describe in English a wide variety of languages according to a single format, thus facilitating comparison and the work of theoretical linguists. A brief introduction is followed by two extensive sections devoted to syntax and morphology, and by a shorter third section on phonology. The first two abound with examples that have accompanying literal glosses in English. Account is taken of dialectal variation.

146 **The Basque language.**
Antonio Tovar, translated by Herbert Pierrepont Houghton.
Philadelphia: University of Pennsylvania Press, 1957. 112p. bibliog.

A translation of Tovar's *La lengua vasca* (1950). The work opens with an outline history of the language and of Basque literature, from a 10th-century inscription to the mid-20th century. This is followed by a survey of the various theories relating Basque to other language groups, including Caucasian, Ural-Altaic, Hamitic, Iberian, Celtic and Romance. Evidence of a relationship with Caucasian languages is considered to be conclusive, while links with putative Iberian are dismissed. There are sections on Basque phonetics, morphology, syntax, vocabulary and dialects.

147 **Basque language survival in rural communities from the Pays Basque, France.**
Raymond Mougeon, Françoise Mougeon. In: *Anglo-American contributions to Basque studies; essays in honor of Jon Bilbao.* Edited by William A. Douglass, Richard W. Etulain, William H. Jacobsen Jr. Reno, Nevada: Desert Research Institute, 1977, p. 107-17. (Desert Research Institute Publications on the Social Sciences, no. 13).

A statistical survey carried out in four mountain villages near St.-Jean-Pied-de-Port in 1976 demonstrates that farming families are the most likely social group to have Basque-speaking children, but that their proportion, compared to French-speaking children, is markedly smaller than among their parents' generation.

148 **Basque phonology.**
José Ignacio Hualde. London; New York: Routledge, 1991. 210p. map. bibliog. (Theoretical Linguistics Series).

Described in the editorial statement as 'the first comprehensive treatment of the phonological system of Basque', this study is of interest to specialist phonologists and Basque linguists.

149 **Basques et géorgiens.** (Basques and Georgians.)
Chota Dzidzigouri. Tbilisi, Georgia: University of Tbilisi, 1983. 259p.

Translated from the original Georgian. The author reviews arguments in favour of a link between the Basques and Iberians and the peoples living in the Caucasus region, and between the Basque language and Kartvelian-Caucasian languages.

150 **Catalan, Gallego, Vascuence. Ensayo bibliográfico de estudios lingüísticos, publicados o realizados en España (1970-1986).**
(Catalan, Galician, Basque. Towards a bibliography of linguistic studies published or carried out in Spain, 1970-86.)
John Stevenson. Sydney: University of New South Wales, School of Spanish and Latin American Studies, 1989. 235p.

The section devoted to Basque contains 1,344 items (books, theses and articles) arranged under twenty-one headings, with cross-references between them. Some of the items in Basque have brief English glosses. There are also more general sections listing bibliographies and works on Hispanic languages in general. Although there are no summaries of the items listed, this is a most valuable piece of work.

151 **Diccionario etimológico de los nombres de los pueblos, villas y
ciudades de Navarra. Apellidos navarros.** (Etymological dictionary
of the names of towns, villages and cities of Navarra. Navarrese
surnames.)
Mikel Belasko. Pamplona, Spain: Pamiela, 1996. 461p. bibliog.
(Ensayo y testimonio, no. 22).

Each entry in Belasko's dictionary comprises up to four possible sections: the first
consists of an etymology for the toponym; the second of a philological commentary,
based on his own conclusions or those of other linguists; the third of popular explanations or folk etymologies; and the fourth of documented earlier forms. The subtitle
'surnames' refers to the fact that the majority of Basque surnames are in fact local
names (i.e. derived from toponyms or referring to geographical features). The introduction is succinct and useful.

152 **Euskal deituren hiztegia = Dictionnaire des patronymes basques =
Diccionario de apellidos vascos.** (Dictionary of Basque surnames.)
Philippe Oyhamburu. Ossas-Suhare, France: Hitzak, 1991. 3 vols.

A more comprehensive work than Michelena's (item no. 143), but less accessible. It
includes some 40,000 name forms, some current, others no longer in use, occurring in
the Basque region itself and also throughout Spain, Spanish America, Béarn and
Gascony. Each entry includes an etymological explanation, mention of the area where
the name is found and the date of its first known occurrence. An index at the head of
each letter links variants to the main entry. The work is in three languages – Basque,
French and Spanish. The introduction explains the distinctiveness of Basque surnames
and some important suffixes, and reviews previous work on Basque surnames.

153 **Euskara Biltzarra = Congreso de la Lengua Vasca = Congrès de la
Langue Basque = Conference on the Basque Language.**
Vitoria-Gasteiz, Spain: Eusko Jaurlaritzaren Argitalpen-Zerbitzu
Nagusia = Servicio Central de Publicaciones, Gobierno Vasco, 1988.
3 vols.

This conference was part of the Second World Basque Conference held in the Spanish
Basque region in 1985. The proceedings contain numerous papers in English. The first
volume contains descriptive studies of grammar, history of the language and phonology.
The second is devoted to the sociolinguistics of Basque and the third to language
acquisition and the teaching of Basque.

154 **Evidence from Basque for a new theory of grammar.**
Esméralda Manandise. New York; London: Garland, 1988. 363p.
bibliog. (Outstanding Dissertations in Linguistics).

An analysis of Gipuzkoan Basque, focusing upon its syntactic structures and the
relationship between them and the morphology of the auxiliary verb system. The
author defines the theory of grammar that she applies as clearly generative, but the
Basque data employed introduces new ideas concerning how arguments are specified
in the language.

155 **Generative studies in Basque linguistics.**
Edited by José Ignacio Hualde, Jon Ortiz de Urbina. Amsterdam;
Philadelphia: John Betjamins Publishing Co., 1993. 333p. (Amsterdam
Studies in the Theory and History of Science. Series IV, Current Issues
in Linguistic Theory, vol. 105).
A collection of twelve highly specialist essays applying theories of generative grammar
to modern Basque.

156 **The history of Basque.**
R. L. Trask. London; New York: Routledge, 1997. 458p. bibliog.
An extremely comprehensive work covering the history of the Basque people, the
grammar and history of the Basque language and its possible connections with other
languages. Previous scholarship is evaluated and many misconceptions concerning
both the grammar and links with other languages are exposed. The central chapters
deal with phonological prehistory, morphology and syntax. A further chapter discusses
the sources of Basque vocabulary and examines specific parts of the lexicon (e.g. parts
of the body, numbers, days of the week). Non-specialists will also benefit from
the sections on personal names and toponyms.

157 **Papers from the Basque Linguistics Seminar. University of
Nevada, Summer, 1972.**
Anuario del Seminario de Filología Vasca, no. 6 (1972), 182p.
A collection of ten specialist papers on specific aspects of Basque grammar, phonology
and dialectology.

158 **Parameters in the grammar of Basque. A GB approach to Basque
syntax.**
Jon Ortiz de Urbina. Dordrecht, the Netherlands: Foris Publications,
1989. 278p. bibliog. (Studies in Generative Grammar, no. 33).
Applies a Government and Binding approach to Basque, demonstrating that such a
framework proves explanatorily adequate for many constructions in the language, just
as it does for better-known languages.

159 **Prologomena to a grammar of Basque.**
Terence H. Wilbur. Amsterdam: John Benjamins, 1979. 188p.
bibliog. (Amsterdam Studies in the Theory and History of Linguistic
Science. Series IV, Current Issues in Linguistic Theory, vol. 8).
Applies recent grammatical theories (e.g. transformational grammar, case grammar) to
the Basque language. As well as seeking to account adequately for the grammar of
Basque, the study also tests the applicability of the particular theories.

160   **The Spanish language, together with Portuguese, Catalan and Basque.**
William J. Entwistle.   London: Faber & Faber, 1962. 2nd ed. 367p.
8 maps. bibliog. (The Great Languages).

First published in 1936, and still, despite its brevity, one of the clearest descriptions in English of the Basque language, its phonology, syntax, vocabulary, its possible links with Iberian (which Entwistle saw as tenuous, but more plausible than the Caucasian theory) and its limited impact on Hispano-Latin and Castilian.

161   **Toponymie basque: noms de pays, communes, hameaux et quartiers historiques de Labourd, Basse-Navarre et Soule.** (Basque toponomy: names of regions, communes, villages and historical quarters of Labourd, Basse Navarre and Soule.)
Jean-Baptiste Orpustan.   Talence, France: Presses Universitaires de Bordeaux, 1990. 194p. 3 maps. (Centre d'Études Linguistiques et Littéraires Basques, no. 1).

A rigorous study of the place-names, both Basque and Romance, of the three French Basque provinces. An etymology of each name is given, based on its earliest documented forms, and its evolution to the present form is traced. The places are also situated in their geographical, historical and social contexts.

162   **Towards a history of the Basque language.**
Edited by José Ignacio Hualde, Joseba A. Lakarra, R. L. Trask.
Amsterdam; Philadelphia: John Benjamins, 1995. 365p. bibliog.
(Amsterdam Studies in the Theory and History of Linguistic Science.
Series IV, Current Issues in Linguistic Theory, vol. 131).

A valuable collection of twelve essays, some incorporating recent research, others translations of important earlier articles. They cover the external history of Basque, its possible relationship to other languages and its phonology, morphology and syntax, from a historical perspective.

Minorités nationales et liturgie romaine. L'exemple de la liturgie en Basque. (National minorities and the Roman Catholic liturgy. The example of the liturgy in Basque.)
See item no. 175.

Reinventing Basque society: cultural difference and the quest for modernity, 1918-1936.
See item no. 193.

Basic law of the standardization of the use of Basque.
See item no. 222.

Dictionaries

163 **Basque-English dictionary.**
Gorka Aulestia. Reno, Nevada: University of Nevada Press, 1989.
558p. bibliog. (The Basque Series).
At present the only reliable major Basque-English dictionary. Its vocabulary reflects the modern world, rather than a traditional rural environment. The word list includes both *batua* (unified Basque) and frequently used words from six dialects. Many examples are given, although arguably some of the illustrations of noun usage are superfluous. The substantial introduction includes verb tables and useful sections on grammar, stress, word order and proper names.

164 **Basque-English, English-Basque dictionary.**
Gorka Aulestia, Linda White. Reno, Nevada: University of Nevada Press, 1992. 669p. map. (The Basque Series).
Based on the two bilingual dictionaries (item nos. 163 and 169), this single volume retains the vast majority of the headwords, but removes all the examples. The Basque-English section occupies some sixty per cent of the book. It is also published in Europe: *Euskara-ingelesa/Ingelesa-euskara hiztegia* (Donostia, Spain: Elkar, 1992).

165 **Diccionario 3000 Hiztegia.** (Dictionary 3000.)
'Bostak Bat' Lantaldea. Bilbo, Spain: 'Bostak Bat' Lantaldea, 1996. 742p., 676p. (Adorez, no. 7).
The most up-to-date Basque-Spanish, Spanish-Basque dictionary, compiled with the practical aims of users in mind. The editors are careful to distinguish different meanings of headwords by the use of synonyms, particularly in the Spanish-Basque section. The Basque-Spanish section includes examples of dialect alongside modern terms, while the Spanish-Basque section prefers translations into *batua* (standardized Basque).

166 **Diccionario etimológico vasco.** (Etymological dictionary of Basque.)
Manuel Agud, Antonio Tovar. Donostia-San Sebastián, Spain: Gipuzkoako Foru Aldundia = Diputación Foral de Guipúzcoa, 1989- . (Anejos del *Anuario del Seminario de Filología Vasca 'Julio de Urquijo'*).
The authors recognized that an etymological dictionary of Basque might have appeared an impossibility given the language's status as an isolate. Nonetheless, the material compiled here is of immense value, as it includes all known dialectal variants and early forms, which are themselves open to internal analysis. In addition, borrowings from Romance languages, Latin and Arabic can be traced and recorded, before the dictionary enters the more hypphothetical territory of non-Romance Indo-European languages and non-Indo-European languages. These last possibilities (no more than phonetic coincidences) are duly included in order to provide a corpus of material on which philologists might draw.

167 **Diccionario general vasco = Orotariko euskal hiztegia.** (General dictionary of Basque.)
Luis Michelena.   Bilbao, Spain: Real Academia de la Lengua Vasca = Euskaltzaindia; Desclée de Brouwer; Ediciones Mensajero, 1987- .
A historical dictionary that aims to record the vocabulary of Basque in all its dialects and from all periods, based on citations from written sources down to 1970. Spanish equivalents are given. Michelena died in 1987 and the project was continued and revised by a team led by Ibon Sarasola. Volume 8 (down to *Kop*) appeared in 1997.

168 **Diccionario Retana de autoridades de la lengua vasca.** (Retana dictionary of authorities in Basque.)
Manuel de la Sota, Pierre Lafitte, Lino de Akesolo.   Bilbao, Spain: La Gran Enciclopedia Vasca, 1976-89. 9 vols. bibliog. (Title on spine: Diccionario Retana de autoridades del euskera.)
A dictionary of authorities, citing usage of Basque words and expressions, including dialectalisms, from so-called 'classical' authors. There are translations into Spanish of headwords, but not of the citations. Dates and texts used are cited in a preliminary bibliography. The work has probably now been surpassed by the *Diccionario general vasco* (no. 167).

169 **English-Basque dictionary.**
Gorka Aulestia, Linda White.   Reno, Nevada; Las Vegas: University of Nevada Press, 1990. 397p. bibliog. (The Basque Series).
Follows on from Aulestia's *Basque-English dictionary* (item no. 163). The smaller size is explained by the reduction in the number of headwords (the companion volume includes five dialects, plus *batua*), and by the regrettable reduction in the size of entries, which rarely distinguish between a number of possible translations. However, it is a pioneering effort and has no competitor.

170 **Oxford photo dictionary. Ingelesa-euskera.** (English-Basque Oxford photo dictionary.)
Oxford: Oxford University Press, 1992. 141p.
Intended for learners of English, this picture dictionary lists objects identified in contemporary English scenes in both Basque and English. Pages are also devoted to wildlife and to particular parts of speech. The dictionary is also of use to English speakers interested in Basque.

Courses

171 **The Basque language. A practical introduction.**
Alan R. King. Reno, Nevada; Las Vegas; London: University of
Nevada Press, 1993. 462p. (The Basque Series).

The forty units of this language course contain dialogues or narratives, relevant
vocabulary and explanatory grammar notes and exercises. It aims to teach the individual
learner or class the basis of Basque, and to provide an insight into the world of the
Basques themselves. It also has a substantial reference section providing further analysis
of all the major grammatical features of the language.

172 **Colloquial Basque. A complete language course.**
Alan R. King, Begotxu Olaizola Elordi. London; New York:
Routledge, 1996. 246p. map.

The only effective introductory course in spoken Basque for English speakers. It is
arranged in twelve units consisting of a Basque text, vocabulary and explanatory notes
in English, supported by brief, straightforward exercises. The course also gives
information about present-day Basque life and culture. The variant of Basque
employed is based on contemporary informal Gipuzkoan speech, supplemented by
some non-conversational passages.

Religion

173 **A Basque challenge to the pre-Civil War Spanish Church.**
Frances Lannon. *European Studies Review*, no. 9 (1979), p. 29-48.
Lannon examines Basque nationalist tendencies and a greater social awareness in the training of priests at the seminary in Vitoria in the 1930s, which contrasted with the rigid, scholastic training that had hitherto prevailed, and which was prevalent elsewhere in Spain. One of the professors behind this movement was the eminent folklorist and priest, José Miguel de Barandiarán, who held the chair of ethnology, prehistory and geology.

174 **Christianity and the Basques.**
Roger Collins. In: *Law, culture and regionalism in early medieval Spain.* Aldershot, England: Variorum, 1992, item IX.
The date of the conversion of the Basques to Christianity has proved impossible to determine with certainty. Oddly, there appear to have been Basque Christians in the late 4th century and pagans in the early 8th century. The paradox could be resolved if the former were townspeople, and the latter mountain dwellers who remained unconverted and culturally different from, and hostile to, city dwellers. This is an English version of Collins's 'El Cristianismo y los habitantes de las montañas en época romana', *Cristianismo y aculturación en tiempos del imperio romano,* edited by Antonio González Blanco and José María Blázquez Martínez, *Antigüedad y cristianismo,* 7 (Murcia, Spain: Universidad de Murcia, 1990 [i.e. 1993]).

175 **Minorités nationales et liturgie romaine. L'exemple de la liturgie en basque.** (National minorities and the Roman Catholic liturgy. The example of the liturgy in Basque.)
J. M. de Lachaga. Paris: Le Centurion, 1979. 286p. bibliog.
Studies the issues surrounding the translation of the Roman Catholic liturgy into Basque following the decision at Vatican II (1963) to use versions in vernacular languages. Lachaga traces the response of the ecclesiastical authorities in the Basque region, and follows the various stages in the production of a Basque version. He also

refers to earlier translations (e.g. Orixe's Missal, published in 1949). The linguistic and theological debates surrounding the Vatican II translation are explored, with particular reference to the debate over the form of language – unified literary or traditional dialects – to be used. (The latter were associated with the more conservative Catholic teachings and views.) The final chapter looks at the response of the Church in the region to new, less hierarchical tendencies, and to the possible formation of a Basque church. The bibliography is especially extensive.

176　**Moving crucifixes in modern Spain.**
William A. Christian Jr.　Princeton, New Jersey: Princeton University Press, 1992. 220p. 3 maps. bibliog.

Visions of moving crucifixes were reported in Spain in the period 1918-22. Christian studies the apparition at Limpias (Santander) in 1919 and subsequent apparitions at Piedramillera and Mañeru in Navarra in 1920. He focuses upon the reported experiences of ordinary people, parish priests and preachers and the subsequent reaction of the Church hierarchy. He sets these events against a background of uncertainty – of conflict between conservative religion on the one hand and Liberalism and anticlericalism on the other.

177　**The religious role of the woman in Basque culture.**
Roslyn M. Frank.　In: *Anglo-American contributions to Basque studies: essays in honor of Jon Bibao.*　Edited by William A. Douglass, Richard W. Etulain, William H. Jacobsen Jr.　Reno, Nevada: Desert Research Institute, 1977, p. 153-58. (Desert Research Institute Publications on the Social Sciences, no. 13).

Explores the position of woman as *serora* (approximates to sacristan) in the everyday life of the Basque church. The role fell into disrepute during the 16th and 17th centuries, when it was seen by the Catholic hierarchy as deviant, even though it was a tradition within the Basque church. Many *serorak* were condemned as witches both in the French and Spanish region.

178　**Visionaries. The Spanish Republic and the reign of Christ.**
William A. Christian Jr.　Berkeley, California; Los Angeles; London: University of California Press, 1996. 544p.

A thoroughly comprehensive and objective account of a series of visions of the Virgin Mary witnessed at Ezkioga (Bizkaia) in 1931. The supporters of the seers were closely linked to both traditional Catholic and Basque nationalist movements and opposed the liberalism of the Second Republic. The growth of opposition, both political and ecclesiastical, to the mystic movement is documented in detail. Separate sections are devoted to the personages involved and their personal histories. Extensive chapters also describe the recurrent patterns of the visions, the kinds of people who experienced them and rational explanations of the phenomena. The Ezkioga visions are placed in the context of similar events elsewhere in Europe after Lourdes, and of other predictions and prophecies.

179 **The witches' advocate. Basque witchcraft and the Spanish Inquisition (1609-1614).**
Gustav Henningsen.   Reno, Nevada: University of Nevada Press, 1980. 607p. map. bibliog. (The Basque Series).

In the early 17th century accusations of witchcraft in the village of Zugarramurdi (Navarra) led to an outbreak of similar accusations elsewhere in the Spanish Basque region, which resulted in a trial and auto-da-fé at Logroño. Drawing on archival evidence, Henningsen examines the behaviour of those who made accusations and those who confessed, and the response of the Inquisition. In particular he examines the work of the inquisitor Alfonso de Salazar, who doubted the truth of the accusations and of the voluntary confessions. Henningsen concludes that there was no cult of witchcraft or heresy, but a fatal combination of the witchcraft theory of theologians, popular beliefs leading to hysteria and the selfish motives of individuals and local authorities.

180 **The world of the witches.**
Julio Caro Baroja, translated from the Spanish by Nigel Glendinning. London: Weidenfeld & Nicolson, 1964. 313p. (The Nature of Human Society Series).

A translation of Caro Baroja's book of 1961 devoted to the history of European witchcraft. He devotes all of Part III and sections of Part IV to the Basque region, providing a narrative account of outbreaks of accusations of witchcraft, the investigations, evidence and conclusions, from the late Middle Ages to the mid-20th century. He deals in particular with the great trials instigated in the Labourd by the judge Pierre de Lancre in the early 17th century, and the subsequent outbreak of accusations of witchcraft in Zugarramurdi and the sceptical conclusions of the inquisitor Alfonso de Salazar.

Social Conditions and Social Organization

General

181 **Atlas etnográfico de Vasconia = Euskalerriko atlas etnografikoa = Atlas ethnographique du Pays Basque.** (Ethnographic atlas of the Basque Country.)
Etniker Euskalerria.   Bilbao, Spain: Etniker Euskalerria; Eusko Jaurlaritza; Gobierno de Navarra, 1990- . maps. bibliog.

The published results of full-scale research into the traditional way of life and social organization of the Basque people. So far three volumes have been published (in Spanish): volume 3: *La alimentación doméstica en Vasconia* (Domestic cooking in the Basque Country); volume 6: *Juegos infantiles en Vasconia* (Children's games in the Basque Country); and vol. 10: *Ritos funerarios en Vasconia* (Funeral rites in the Basque Country).

182 **Borderland influences in a Navarrese village.**
William A. Douglass.   In: *Anglo-American contributions to Basque studies: essays in honor of Jon Bilbao.*   Edited by William A. Douglass, Richard W. Etulain, William H. Jacobsen Jr.   Reno, Nevada: Desert Research Institute, 1977, p. 135-44. (Desert Research Institute Publications on the Social Sciences, no. 13).

Taking as his starting-point David Gómez-Ibáñez's study of life in the Western Pyrenees and the impact of the national boundary (item no. 37), Douglass explores how associations have existed across the border in the form of political refugees and draft dodgers, smuggling, grazing rights and hunting.

183 **Los vascos.** (The Basques.)
Julio Caro Baroja. Madrid: Ediciones Minotauro, 1958. 2nd ed. 540p.
(España en su historia, no. 2).

A revised and updated version of this fundamental work, first published in 1949. Caro Baroja analyses the development of population centres, from antiquity down to the modern age, in both the French and Spanish regions, devoting subsequent chapters to agricultural, fishing, mining and commercial communities. He also studies the practices of naming houses, family and neighbourhood structures, religious beliefs, witchcraft, the arts and other recreations, including sport. The final chapter includes a most useful summary of Basque social evolution, divided into eleven periods or 'cycles' from prehistory to the present, under the following headings: social institutions; economy; technology; magic and religion; and art and language. This important book has been reprinted most recently by Istmo (Madrid, 1995).

The French Region

184 **Basque conflict management choices.**
M. E. R. Nicholson. In: *Essays in Basque social anthropology and history.* Edited by William A. Douglass. Reno, Nevada: Basque Studies Program, University of Nevada, 1989, p. 81-105. (Basque Studies Program Occasional Paper Series, no. 4).

Studies the use of non-confrontational methods (e.g. mediation) to resolve internal disputes in French Basque society, and law as a means of preserving social unity. Confrontational methods are frequently employed in resolving conflict with external forces.

185 **The circle of mountains. A Basque shepherding community.**
Sandra Ott. Oxford: Clarendon Press, 1981. 238p. 3 maps. bibliog. Reissued, Reno, Nevada; London: University of Nevada Press, 1993.

An ethnographic study of the commune of Sainte-Engrâce in the French province of Soule. Ott first describes the historical, environmental and socio-economic context of the community and its three basic social institutions – the household, the Church and 'first neighbours'. The ordering principle of this last, a group of neighbours providing mutual assistance, is one of co-operation and reciprocity. This same principle underlies the organization of the cheese-making syndicates and of shepherds' mountain huts. Ott identifies two further organizing principles, alternation and rotation, present in the human activity of the community.

The Spanish Region

186   **Baserria.** (The Basque farmhouse.)
Alberto Santana, photographs by Xabi Otero.   Donostia-San
Sebastián, Spain: Gipuzkoako Foru Aldundia, Kultura eta Turismo
Saila = Diputación Foral de Gipuzkoa, Departamento de Cultura y
Turismo, 1993. 108p. bibliog. (Bertan, no. 4).
The *baserria* is at the core of Basque rural life. This study touches on the history of
farming in Gipuzkoa, different kinds of houses and the way of life. The importance of
the indivisibility of inheritance in the Basque region, a factor that has led to emigration,
is also covered. The photographs are excellent and the English translation of the original
Basque text is appended.

187   **Basque violence. Metaphor and sacrament.**
Joseph Zulaika.   Reno, Nevada; Las Vegas: University of Nevada
Press, 1984. 423p. map. bibliog. (The Basque Series).
An anthropological approach to events surrounding six murders in Itziar (Gipuzkoa) in
1975, five (one a blunder) by ETA and one by the Civil Guard. Zulaika draws on the
testimonies and recollections of individual villagers, and seeks to contextualize the
political violence in Basque society, relating it to other socio-cultural manifestations
in the rural community, including popular games, hunting and *bertsolaritza*. The work
should not be seen as an apology for terrorism, but as a possible explanation of the
dynamics of violence.

188   **Death in Murélaga. Funerary ritual in a Spanish Basque village.**
William A. Douglass.   Seattle, Washington; London: University of
Washington Press, 1969. 240p. bibliog. (Monograph 49/The American
Ethnological Society).
This anthropological study of customs in rural Bizkaia in 1965-66 passes from a
description of the customs themselves to an examination of the different roles in these
proceedings of the family, household (i.e. the residential unit) and neighbourhood of
the deceased. It thus reveals the nature and basis of an isolated community's social
organization. The effect of a death on each of the three social units is examined in
terms of its impact on human relationships and in economic terms.

189   **Echalar and Murelaga. Opportunity and rural exodus in two
Spanish Basque villages.**
William A. Douglass.   London: C. Hurst, 1975. 222p. map.
Douglass compares and contrasts two rural, apparently similar communities at the
start of this century, one in Navarra (Echalar), the other in Bizkaia (Murélaga), both
consisting of smallholdings engaged in mixed farming. He charts social, economic and
demographic changes from 1900 to the mid-1970s. Echalar reveals a marked rural
exodus, while the population of Murélaga has remained relatively stable. Both
communties have suffered a crisis in agriculture prompted by industrialization. The
former now depends upon machines and is affected by national economic factors. The
second now relies heavily upon pinewood production.

190 **Informe sobre la situación de las mujeres en Euskadi.** (Report on the position of women in Euskadi.)
Emakunde = Instituto Vasco de la Mujer. Vitoria-Gasteiz: Emakunde = Instituto Vasco de la Mujer; Gobierno Vasco, Departamento de Interior, Dirección de Procesos Electorales y Documentación, 1991. 168 + 168p. bibliog.

Examines the contemporary social position of women in the Basque Autonomous Community in terms of education, employment (including salary levels), health, social issues (old age, violence against women, drug addiction, prostitution), and political participation. It utilizes existing surveys, statistics and current legislation and draws comparisons with other countries. There is a parallel text in Spanish and Basque.

191 **Las mujeres en la Comunidad Autónoma de Euskadi.** (Women in the Autonomous Community of Euskadi.)
Emakunde = Instituto Vasco de la Mujer. Vitoria-Gasteiz, Spain: Emakunde = Instituto Vasco de la Mujer, 1992. 158 + 158p. (Informe, no. 3).

Presents findings and statistics evidencing the social disadvantage of women in Euskadi. Not surprisingly, the results show the perpetuation of traditional family roles and forms of employment, and unequal participation in education, politics, etc. The other issues covered are as in the *Informe* (no. 190).

192 **The position of women in a Basque fishing community.**
Charlotte Crawford. In: *Anglo-American contributions to Basque studies: essays in honor of Jon Bilbao.* Edited by William A. Douglass, Richard W. Etulain and William H. Jacobson Jr. Reno, Nevada: Desert Research Institute, 1977, p. 145-52. (Desert Research Institute Publications on the Social Sciences, no. 13).

Presents portraits of three women members of a Basque fishing family in Bermeo (Bizkaia). The author explores the nature of so-called matriarchy, its values, attitudes and areas of influence, and concludes that this sector of Basque society is itself neither matrilineal nor matriarchal, but that Basque families are 'matrifocal' (i.e. women occupy a strong position within them).

193 **Reinventing Basque society: cultural difference and the quest for modernity, 1918-1936.**
Jacqueline Urla. In: *Essays in Basque social anthropology and history.* Edited by William A. Douglass. Reno, Nevada: Basque Studies Program, 1989, p. 149-76. (Basque Studies Program Occasional Papers Series, no. 4).

A valuable study of the aims of Eusko Ikaskuntza or Sociedad de Estudios Vascos (Basque Studies Society), founded in 1918, and responsible for preparing the first Basque statute of autonomy. Urla's article focuses on the twin aims of preserving cultural identity and modernizing society, charting how nationalist concern for racial purity gave way to emphasis on language modernization and unification, and how the Society promulgated social reform through health care, social insurance and savings schemes.

194 **Serving girls and sheepherders: emigration and continuity in a Spanish Basque village.**
William A. Douglass.   In: *The changing faces of rural Spain.*   Edited by Joseph B. Aceves, William A. Douglass.   Cambridge, Massachusetts: Schenkman Publishing Co.; New York; London: John Wiley, 1976, p. 45-51.

Emigration has been a demographic feature of traditional Basque smallholdings this century, particularly since 1945. Douglass examines the contrasting expectations of men and women who left Echalar to work as shepherds or lumberjacks, or as domestics. The men hope to return to farming, while the women opt to stay on in a town or city, thus reducing the number of potential marriage partners and, indirectly, the number of small farms.

Politics

General

195 **Basque politics. A case study in ethnic nationalism.**
Edited by William A. Douglass. Reno, Nevada: Associated Faculty
Press and Basque Studies Program, 1985. 334p. (Basque Studies
Program Occasional Papers Series, no. 2).

A collection of eleve ssays analysing issues surrounding Basque nationalism from
the 16th century to the present. The following are all reproduced in books (items nos.
109, 120, 187, 201, 205, 209, 218 and 220): Jacob on the loss of Basque rights and
traditions in France during the Revolution; Barahona on the defence of the *fueros* and
privileges against a Liberal central government in 1820; Legarreta on the international
response to the appeal for help for Basque refugee children; Payne on 20th-century
Navarrese nationalism; Clark on Basque political attitudes in the post-Franco era;
Zirakzadeh on the politics of Basque businessmen; Heiberg on political divisions in
Gipuzkoa; and Zulaika on the death of a presumed informer. Three additional articles
are based on their authors' work in Spanish. Gregorio Monreal (p. 19-49) examines
conflicting views on the status of Basque *fueros* in 16th-century Basque political
thought, which were seen as concessions by centrists but as codifications of rights by
nationalist historians. Vicente Garmendia (p. 137-53) analyses the intellectual background to Carlist thought at the time of the Second Carlist War, and how this later
developed into Basque nationalism. José Luis de la Granja (p. 155-73) examines the
failure of the Basque nationalist movement to establish (through the Nationalist Party)
political hegemony throughout the region, especially in Alava and Navarra, and to
represent working-class views and right-wing conservatives.

196 The Basques: their struggle for independence.
Luis Núñez Astrain, translated from the French by Meic Stephens with an introduction by Ned Thomas. Caernarfon[?], Wales: Welsh Academic Press, 1997. 165p.

First published as *La razón vasca* (Tafalla, Spain: Txalaparta, 1995). Núñez Astrain, editor-in-chief of the Basque-language daily *Egin*, cogently articulates the nationalist interpretation of the Basques' history and their present situation, from the standpoint of the right to self-determination. In the introduction he clearly demonstrates how a people is split between two countries, three areas of local administration and other secular (and religious) authorities.

197 Diccionario histórico-político de Euskal Herria. (Historico-political dictionary of the Basque Country.)
Iñaki Egaña. Tafalla, Spain: Txalaparta, 1996. 758p. (Colección Orreaga, 34-35).

Contains some 700 entries embracing a very wide range of subjects. In addition to useful explanations such as *abertzalea* (nationalist, independentist left), brief biographies of cultural figures (e.g. Antoine d'Abbadie) and political alliances (e.g. the Pact of Ajuria Enea, 1988), there are paragraphs on Jesus Christ, the Ku Klux Klan and sexuality!

198 Guerrilla and terrorist organizations: a world directory and bibliography.
Peter Janke, with Richard Sim. Brighton, England: Harvester Press, 1983. 531p. 7 maps.

Chapters on France and Spain list Basque terrorist organizations and give brief accounts of their history and motivation. It is useful due to its inclusion of information on less well-known groups, e.g. the French Euzkal Zuzentasuna (Basque Justice), and right-wing groups, e.g. Batallón Vasco Español (Spanish Basque Battalion).

199 Linguistic minorities in Western Europe.
Meic Stephens. Llandysul, Dyfed, Wales: Gomer Press, 1976. 796p. bibliog.

Stephens devotes two sections to the Basques, to those in the French region (p. 317-27) and to those living in Spain (p. 633-64), from a distinctly pro-nationalist perspective. The section on Spain concentrates on the repression of language and culture and on politics towards the end of the Franco period. This latter account is useful, as is Stephens' summary of the attitude of the Catholic Church in the region, especially its priests, towards the Franco régime. The section on the Pays Basque points out the markedly less militant attitude of French Basque nationalists, while stressing the centrist nature of French governments and various acts of repression that have taken place since the suppression of autonomy in Soule and Labourd and the creation of the department of Basses-Pyrénées in 1790. He highlights the predominantly cultural nature of the nationalist movements of recent years.

200 **The roots of identity. Three national movements in contemporary European politics.**
Patricia Elton Mayo.   London: Allen Lane, 1974. 171p.

Mayo devotes five chapters to the Basque region. The chapters on the future of the Basques and 'the position today' in the Spanish region have been overtaken by events. However, the chapters on the French region are more useful, as less has been written about them in English. 'The position today' in France highlights the work of the nationalist group, Enbata, and clarifies the position of the central government in its relations with Spain over Basque refugees. The final chapter on the economic situation of the French region is also especially welcome.

The French Region

201 **Hills of conflict. Basque nationalism in France.**
James E. Jacob.   Reno, Nevada; Las Vegas; London: University of Nevada Press, 1994. 546p. bibliog. (The Basque Series).

A history of resistance to the central government in France, from the Ancien Régime to the early 1990s, heavily weighted toward the post-1960 period. It chronicles the separation of nationalism from the conservatism of Catholicism and the concomitant rise of secular radicalism. Analysis of the latter's relationship to the Basque separatist movement ETA reveals the divisions in the French Basque movement over the use of violence. Also particularly useful is the examination of the divergent attitudes taken by French Basques to Germany during the Second World War and how best to advance the Basque cause. Jacob's bibliography is especially extensive.

Activités en Pays Basque. Commerce, industrie, tourisme. Revue mensuelle. (Activities in the Pays Basque. Commerce, industry, tourism. Monthly magazine.)
See item no. 241.

The Spanish Region

202 **At play with identity in the Basque arena.**
Jeremy MacClancy.   In: *Inside European identities. Ethnography in Western Europe.*   Edited by Sharon Macdonald.   Providence, Rhode Island; Oxford: Berg, 1993, p. 84-97. (Ethnic Identity Series).

Identifies the socially symbolic behaviour that signifies adherence to radical Basque (*abertzale*) nationalism (e.g. attendance at rallies, taunting the national police and a liking for 'radical' Basque rock music). MacClancy goes on to analyse the tension between Basque nationalists in Navarra, supporters of Herri Batasuna and Navarrese nationalists.

203 The Basque Country. The national question and the socialist revolution.

José María Arenillas. Leeds, England: National Administrative Council, Independent Labour Party, [1973?], 27p. 2 maps. (I.L.P. Square One pamphlet).

An English translation of the Spanish original (published in *La nueva era*, Barcelona, 1937) by a member of the Spanish Workers Marxist Unification Party (POUM) who was murdered by Stalinists late in the Spanish Civil War. It highlights the divergent policies of the workers' militias and the conservative Basque Nationalists whose government of 1936 is here seen as essentially betraying the revolutionary movement and handing victory to Franco's rebels.

204 The Basque insurgents: ETA, 1952-1980.

Robert P. Clark. Madison, Wisconsin; London: University of Wisconsin Press, 1984. 328p. 6 maps. bibliog.

Continues his earlier *The Basques: the Franco years and beyond* (no. 209). Clark first analyses the political and economic causes of Basque militancy and the subsequent emergence of ETA. Chapters one to four are a chronological history of the terrorist movement, its ideological evolution, its various groups and their activities. The remaining chapters analyse the nature of terrorist attacks: targets and locale; the profile of terrorists and the manner of their recruitment; the level of support among the Basque population as a whole; and the internal organization and resourcing of ETA's members.

205 Basque nationalism.

Stanley G. Payne. Reno, Nevada: University of Nevada Press, 1975. 291p. map. bibliog. (The Basque Series).

A lucid account of the relationship of the three Spanish Basque Provinces and Navarra with Spanish governments, from the medieval period to the 1970s. It charts the extent of local autonomy and tax exemption until the 1870s, and the subsequent emergence of modern nationalism under the leadership of Sabino Arana y Goiri. Payne further identifies the uneasy relationship in the 20th century between the conservatism and Catholicism of the Partido Nacionalista Vasco (Basque Nationalist Party, founded in 1895) and socialism.

206 The Basques.

Kenneth Medhurst. London: Minority Rights Group, 1972. 24p. (Report/Minority Rights Group, no. 9).

Summarizes the origins of Basque nationalism and gives an account of the society and politics of the Spanish Basque region, the state of the Basque language and forms of state repression towards the end of the Franco era.

207 **Basques, anti-Basques and the moral community.**
Marianne Heiberg. In: *'Nation' and 'state' in Europe.*
Anthropological perspectives. Edited by R. D. Grillo. London:
Academic Press, 1980, p. 45-59.
Defines the shifting difference between Basques and anti- (or non-) Basques during
two periods: the birth of nationalism in the 1890s; and its re-emergence in the 1960s.
The earlier nationalism defined 'Basque' in terms of race, the second, in terms of
culture. The first excluded socialism, and the second encouraged it in spite of the
political contradictions and oppositions it entailed between conservatives and radicals.

208 **The Basques, the Catalans and Spain. Alternative routes to
nationalist mobilisation.**
Daniele Conversi. London: Hurst & Co., 1997. 312p. 7 maps.
bibliog.
In spite of economic and political similarities between the two regions, Basque and
Catalan nationalism evolved very differently. Conversi focuses on differences in class
structure, wealth distribution and cultural vitality, which have produced an integra-
tionist Catalan national culture, and an exclusive Basque one. Basque society is not
seen as essentially violent: ETA's militancy and terrorism is seen as stemming from
the absence of a fully coherent cultural and political programme and the harshness of
state repression.

209 **The Basques: the Franco years and beyond.**
Robert P. Clark. Reno, Nevada: University of Nevada Press, 1979.
434p. 3 maps. bibliog. (The Basque Series).
A historical account of Basque nationalism, from its beginnings in the late 19th
century until 1978, when the Spanish Constitution was approved and the Statute of
Autonomy was drafted. Clark concentrates upon the beginnings of clandestine Basque
resistance after the Spanish Civil War, and on the emergence of four distinct forms of
resistance: political (the Basque Nationalist Party); linguistic (the *ikastolak*); revolutionary (ETA); and economic (national and Basque trade unions). He concludes with
the period of transition to democracy, continued ETA violence and an analysis of
voting patterns in the Basque region in the 1977 national elections.

210 **Big business and the rise of Basque nationalism.**
Joseph Harrison. *European Studies Review*, no. 7 (1977), p. 371-91.
Focuses upon the brief 'Indian summer' at the end of the First World War when the
Bizkaian business élite joined forces with the Basque Nationalist Party to oppose
the taxation measures of the central government and seek greater autonomy for the
Spanish Basque region. Hitherto, the greater part of the business class had supported
the Madrid government and they did so again as labour unrest increased in the early
1920s.

211 **Divided nations. Class, politics, and nationalism in the Basque Country and Catalonia.**
Juan Díez Medrano.   Ithaca, New York; London: Cornell University Press, 1995. 236p. bibliog. (The Wilder House Series in Politics, History and Culture).
An analysis of the distinct forms of nationalism that have emerged in the Spanish Basque region and in Catalonia from the end of the 19th century to the present. The distinction is related to differences in patterns of capitalist development, in the type of economy, in the relationship of the ruling élites to Spanish influence and in the class composition of the nationalist groups.

212 **ETA and Basque nationalism. The fight for Euskadi 1890-1986.**
John Sullivan.   London; New York: Routledge, 1988. 299p. bibliog.
A detailed account of the complex history of the terrorist movement and its various factions, seen in relation to nationalism and class struggle. Sullivan usefully elucidates the contradictions in the position of both the traditional and militant wings of the nationalist movement, and he lays bare the myth of a Basque Golden Age of freedom and democracy preceding the Carlist Wars. His explanation of the strength of the armed nationalist movement and his assessment of its viability are clear and judicious. The bibliography is full and there are useful summary charts of ETA's factions and the composition of the nationalist groupings.

213 **Euskadi eta askatasuna = Euskal Herria y la libertad.** (Euskadi and liberty.)
Tafalla, Spain: Txalaparta, 1993-94. 8 vols. 4 videocassettes.
A detailed history of the terrorist group ETA from 1952 until 1992, amply illustrated and containing the text of original documents and newspaper articles. The perspective is militantly nationalist. The text is mainly in Spanish, but some interviews, biographies and many picture captions are in Basque.

214 **Euskal Autonomi Elkarteko Hauteskundeetako datuen biltegia = Data-bank of elections in the Basque Autonomous Community.**
Gobierno Vasco, Departamento de Interior, Dirección de Procesos Electorales y Documentación.   [Vitoria-Gasteiz, Spain]: Eusko Jaurlaritza, Herrizaingo Saila, Hauteskunde eta Dokumentazio Zuzendaritza = Gobierno Vasco, Departamento de Interior, Dirección de Procesos Electorales y Documentación, [1993-96]. 1 booklet, 28 diskettes.
Contains the official results on diskette of all elections in the Autonomous Community from 1977 until the General Election of 1996. It also includes information about political parties and coalition groupings that contested elections. The programme enables more detailed information to be generated. The booklet is in Basque, Spanish, French and English.

215   **GAC: militant Carlist activism, 1968-1972.**
Jeremy MacClancy.   In: *Essays in Basque social anthropology and history.*   Edited by William A. Douglass.   Reno, Nevada: Basque Studies Program, University of Nevada, 1989, p. 177-85. (Basque Studies Program Occasional Papers, no. 4).
GAC (Grupos de Acción Carlistas, or Carlist Action Groups), comprised militant nationalists of the Carlist party, by then left-of-centre and opposed to the Franco régime. They established contacts with ETA and carried out a number of acts of terrorism of limited impact. They had ceased to exist by late 1973.

216   **Historical approaches to nationalism in Spain.**
Xosé M. Núñez Seixas.   Saarbrücken, Germany; Fort Lauderdale, Florida: Breitenbach, 1993. 167p. bibliog. (Forschungen zu Spanien, no. 13).
This critical survey of the historiography of nationalism in Spain is most useful for elucidating how the different nationalisms have been assessed and for its bibliography. The section on Basque nationalism is on p. 81-104.

217   **Immigrants and nationalists: ethnic conflict and accommodation in Catalonia, the Basque Country, Latvia and Estonia.**
Gershon Shafir.   Albany, New York: State University of New York Press, 1995. 279p. maps. bibliog.
Shafir examines and compares the reception of a large influx of immigrants into four regions of Europe that are relatively well-developed economically and have strong nationalist movements and cultures of their own. Concerning the Basque region, he charts the shift from a racial nationalism to a socialist one.

218   **The making of the Basque nation.**
Marianne Heiberg.   Cambridge, England: Cambridge University Press, 1989. 263p. 3 maps. bibliog. (Cambridge Studies in Social Anthropology, no. 66).
Heiberg examines the creation of Basque nationhood out of different social elements: urban and industrial; agricultural; modernizing; and conservative. She also devotes a substantial section to analysing local politics in the village of Elgeta (Gipuzkoa) during the period of transition from dictatorship to democracy (1975-77). In a post-script she argues that the establishment of the autonomous government in 1980 effectively realized many nationalist aspirations in cultural, administrative, and even economic, terms. However, many Basques still aspire to self-determination, although only the 'intransigent' nationalists of Herri Batasuna and ETA remain determinedly excluded from the political process.

219 **Negotiating with ETA. Obstacles to peace in the Basque Country,
1975-1988.**
Robert P. Clark. Reno, Nevada; Las Vegas: University of Nevada
Press, 1990. 278p. map. bibliog. (The Basque Series).
An examination of the nearly thirty attempts to achieve a negotiated settlement
between Spanish governments and the terrorist group ETA. Clark also examines the
anti-terrorist policies both of Spain and France and the clandestine activities of
vigilantes and mercenaries, such as GAL (Grupos Antiterrorista de Liberación = Anti-
Terrorist Liberation Groups). He concludes with an analysis of the numerous failed
negotiations, including issues of principle, such as the right to self-determination, and
the status of terrorists. Useful information on the stakeholders is included (ETA and
its various factions, political parties, and Spanish government ministries and departments).

220 **A rebellious people. Basques, protests, and politics.**
Cyrus Ernesto Zirakzadeh. Reno, Nevada; Las Vegas: University of
Nevada Press, 1991. 260p. bibliog. (The Basque Series).
Adopts a view of political protest in the Spanish region broader than that of ETA's
campaigns, studying non-violent neighbourhood associations and labour organizations.
Zirakzadeh challenges the view that rapid modernization led to a socio-cultural crisis,
seeing instead acute economic grievances in both rural and urban areas. He also discusses the response of ETA to the views of both the neighbourhood associations and
organized labour, and the conflicting pro- and anti-industrialization currents within the
Basque Nationalist Party. ETA's adoption of violence is seen as strongly influenced
by violent revolutionary movements abroad.

Basque violence. Metaphor and sacrament.
See item no. 187.

**Spain. The question of torture. Documents exchanged by Amnesty
International & the Government of Spain.**
See item no. 228.

They shall *not* pass. The autobiography of La Pasionaria.
See item no. 271.

Government and Administration

221 **Euskal Autonomi Elkarteko administrazio-zerbitzuen gidaliburua = Guía de servicios administrativos de la Comunidad Autónoma de Euskadi.** (Guide to the administrative services of the Autonomous Community of Euskadi.)
Vitoria-Gasteiz, Spain: Servicio Central de Publicaciones del Gobierno Vasco, 1993. 1 vol.

The latest edition of a comprehensive guide to the departments of the Basque Government and their subordinate and related bodies. The primary responsibilities and position within the overall organization of each body are indicated, together with their addresses. There are indexes, organized according to the nature of the service (e.g. tourism), by location of offices open to the public and by name of body and subject.

The Basque Country. A social and economic guide.
See item no. 23.

Euskal Herriko Autonomia Estatutoa = Estatuto de autonomía del País Vasco. (Statute of Autonomy of the Basque Country.)
See item no. 224.

Jaurlaritzaren legea = Ley de gobierno. (Law of government.)
See item no. 225.

Law

222 **Basic law on the standardization of the use of Basque.**
Basque Government, Secretariat of Linguistic Policy.   Vitoria-
Gasteiz, Spain: Basque Government, Central Publications Office, 1986.
20p.
The text of a law setting out the role of Basque as an official language within the
Basque Autonomous Community. This law included *inter alia*: the right of students to
be taught in Basque; a citizen's right to be informed and receive communications (TV,
radio) in Basque; the absence of discrimination by using Basque; the use of both
Basque and Spanish in all official texts; and the promotion of Basque by the government. Some clauses on the preferential use of Basque were subsequently declared
unconstitutional.

223 **The Economic Agreement = L'Accord économique.**
Vitoria-Gasteiz, Spain: Basque Government = Gouvernement Basque,
1988. 173p.
The text of the Economic Agreement between the Spanish government and the Basque
Autonomous Community (approved by law May 13 1981) which agreed the tax-raising
powers of the latter. Various amendments in the light of the introduction of VAT
(1985) are also included.

224 **Euskal Herriko Autonomia estatutoa = Estatuto de autonomía del
País Vasco.** (Statute of Autonomy of the Basque Country.)
Vitoria-Gasteiz, Spain: Eusko Jaurlaritzaren-Argitalpen Zerbitzu
Nagusia = Servicio Central de Publicaciones del Gobierno Vasco,
1981. 81p. (Legeliburu bilduma = Colección Textos legales, no. 1).
The law passed by Spanish Parliament (18 December 1979) approving the Statute of
Autonomy for the provinces of Alava, Bizkaia and Gipuzkoa, and admitting Navarra
also if that province so decided. The Statute affirmed the nationality of the Basques
and the official status of the Basque and Spanish languages.

225 **Jaurlaritzaren legea = Ley de gobierno.** (Law of government.)
[Vitoria-Gasteiz, Spain]: Eusko Jaurlaritzaren Argitalpen-Zerbitzu
Nagusia = Servicio Central de Publicaciones del Gobierno Vasco,
1981. 85p. (Legeliburu bilduma = Colección Textos legales, no. 3).

The law passed (30 June 1981) by the Basque Parliament approving the setting up of
the Basque Government, the election of the *lehendakari* (President) and the extent of
the latter's powers and those of other members of the Government. The law also
determined the relationship between Government and Parliament, and the broad
outlines of the administration of the Autonomous Community.

226 **Legislación de Navarra, 1990-** . (Legislation of Navarra, 1990- .)
Pamplona, Spain: Aranzadi, 1991- . (Legislación de las Comunidades
Autónomas).

Contains similar material to item no. 227, except that legislation published in the
official gazette of Navarra replaces that of the three Basque Provinces.

227 **Legislación del País Vasco, 1988-** . (Legislation of the Basque
Country, 1988- .)
Pamplona, Spain: Aranzadi, 1989- . (Legislación de las Comunidades
Autónomas).

An annual publication in Spanish only that includes all legislation in the order that it
appears in the *Boletín oficial* and *Diario oficial* (Official Gazette) of the Basque
Autonomous Community, as well as royal decrees that appear in the *Boletín oficial del
estado* (Spanish Official Gazette) and legislation published in the official gazettes of
the three Basque Provinces. There are comprehensive indexes.

228 **Spain. The question of torture. Documents exchanged by Amnesty
International & the Government of Spain.**
Amnesty International. London: Amnesty International Publications,
1985. 59p.

An Amnesty International mission to Spain in 1983 found evidence of torture of
detainees held incommunicado under anti-terrorist legislation. Some of these detainees
were held in the Basque region. The introduction chronicles Amnesty's dealings with
the Spanish Government and reproduces the memorandum to the Government, the
Minister of the Interior's response and translations of three laws on terrorism, detention
and *habeas corpus* procedure respectively. Amnesty International was unconvinced by
the subsequent provisions in Spanish law for protecting detainees following their initial
memorandum, and remained concerned about the perpetuation of incommunicado
detention.

Economy and Finance

Early period

229　**Money, prices, and wages in Valencia, Aragon, and Navarre, 1351-1500.**
Earl J. Hamilton.　Cambridge, Massachusetts: Harvard University Press, 1936. 310p. bibliog. (Harvard Economic Studies, no. 51).

According to the author, the medieval kingdom of Navarre maintained the best system of public book-keeping of all the Peninsular kingdoms. Thus, relatively comprehensive records of the financial affairs of the royal household have survived. Hamilton draws upon these almost exclusively for his statistics relating both to prices and to wages. The first of his chapters on Navarre deals with the issues of coinage and monetary policy until approximately 1480.

The French Region

230　**La economía de Aquitania desde la perspectiva del País Vasco.**
(The economy of Aquitaine from a Spanish Basque perspective.)
Koldo Hualde.　Vitoria-Gasteiz, Spain: Eusko Jaurlaritza, Ekonomia eta Egitamugintza Saila = Gobierno Vasco, Departamento de Economía y Planificación, 1989. 129p. bibliog. (Serie Documentos de economía, no. 1).

A study intended to make better known in the Basque Autonomous Community the economic situation of the Aquitaine region. In spite of similarities in size of population as a proportion of the total for Spain and France, the two regions are very different.

The Basque Autonomous Community is heavily industrialized, whereas Aquitaine is still predominantly rural with a disproportionately low percentage of France's GDP. The various individual sections of the report examine Aquitaine's agriculture, fishing, manufacturing and service industries.

231   **Pays Basque: économie et société en mutation.** (The Pays Basque: economic and social change.)
Pierre Laborde.   Donostia, Spain; Bayonne, France: Elkar, 1994. 293p.
Examines economic and social change in the French Basque Region this century, focusing on the period from the 1970s until the present. It deals with the development of tourism, the faltering introduction of industry, the consequent shift of population from the interior to the coast and subsequent changes in agricultural techniques and practice. (Agriculture still dominates land use in the region, however.) It also examines the impact of the two World Wars and the oil crisis of 1977.

232   **Le Pays Basque en perspective.** (The Pays Basque in perspective.)
Club de Prospective Pays Basque 2010.   Bayonne, France: Pays Basque 2010, 1994. 91p. map.
An analysis of the present socio-economic situation of the French Basque Region, and its problems, which include an ageing and dwindling population, population shift from rural interior to urban coast, environmental pressures and the state of the Basque language. A range of possible future scenarios and solutions is proposed.

233   **Problèmes du développement économique en Pays Basque Nord.**
(Problems of economic developement in the northern Basque Region.)
Jean Suhubiette, Michel Leizagoyen.   Anglet, France: M. Leizagoyen, 1975. 96p. 2 maps. bibliog.
Prompted by devolutionary measures, introduced in 1972, which created regional assemblies with a consultative role in matters of economic and social development, the authors present a series of economic indicators and infrastructural factors for the Aquitaine region. When ethnic ties are taken into consideration, these factors suggest that the linking of the French and Spanish Basque regions would form a more viable economic area.

The Spanish Region

234   **Basque Country.**
Alan Robinson.   *World Link* (London), (Nov.-Dec. 1994), p. 91-99.
Although events have moved on, Robinson presents a useful overview of the strategy of the government of the Basque Autonomous Community in 1992-93 for revitalizing the economy: diversifying industries; encouraging foreign investment; increasing exports; technological modernization; and investment in infrastructure. Some success stories (e.g. the aerospace industry, railway rolling stock construction and machine tools) are cited.

235   **The Basque Country: an industrial region.**
Focus on Spain (Madrid), no. 6 (Dec. 1995), p. 47-51.
A brief summary of the state of the economy of the Basque Autonomous Community,
covering imports and exports, foreign investment, the machine tool industry, research
and development and government stock issues.

236   **La economía navarra en 1991, etc.** (The Navarrese economy in 1991,
etc.)
Gobierno de Navarra, Servicio de Economía, Sección de Análisis y
Programación.   Pamplona, Spain: Gobierno de Navarra,
Departamento de Economía y Hacienda, 1992[?]- .
Sets the Navarrese economy in the context of the international and the Spanish
economies. Statistics cover production, internal demand, external trade, labour market,
consumer prices, industrial costs, investment and public sector expenditure.

237   **Euskadiko K.A.ko kontu ekonomikoak = Cuentas económicas de la
C. A. de Euskadi, 1982- .** (Economic accounts of the Autonomous
Community of Euskadi, 1982- .)
Gobierno Vasco, Dirección de Estadística.   [Vitoria-Gasteiz, Spain]:
Eusko Jaurlaritza = Gobierno Vasco, [1985?]- .
Presents a summary of total economic activity in Euskadi and accounts for public
administration at the level of both the Basque Government and the provincial adminis-
trations. Economic indicators, including price levels and turnover across a range of
industries, are also included. Issues since 1984 have been published by the Instituto
Vasco de Estadística, later known generally as EUSTAT. With the 1988 issue the title
changed to *Kontu ekonomikoak = Cuentas económicas.*

238   **Informe anual integrado de la Hacienda Vasca, 1989- .** (Annual
integrated report of the Basque Treasury, 1989- .)
[Vitoria-Gasteiz, Spain]: Órgano de Coordinación Tributaria de
Euskadi, 1990 [i.e. 1991]- .
Includes a description of the tax-raising powers of the Basque Autonomous Community and its responsibility for payment of taxes to the central government, agreed
after the *Ley de concierto económico* (Law of economic agreement) of 1981 and the
Ley de armonización, coordinación y colaboración fiscal (Law on tax harmonization,
coordination and collaboration) of 1989. Each issue summarizes the taxes (value-
added, corporation and personal) paid by each of the three Basque Provinces.

239   **Observatorio económico = Euskal ekonomi koiuntura. Informe
1987- .** (Economic monitor. Report 1987- .)
Gobierno Vasco, Departamento de Economía y Planificación,
Dirección de Coyuntura y Planificación Económica.   Vitoria-Gasteiz,
Spain: Gobierno Vasco, Servicio Central de Publicaciones, 1988- .
Sets the economy of the Basque Autonomous Community in its international, Spanish
and regional context. The 1990 edition reviews industrial and overseas trade statistics
for the period 1988-90. It also surveys the labour market, consumer and industrial

prices, the performance of the public sector and foreign investment. The 1990 edition has the Spanish title *Observatorio económico de coyuntura vasca.*

The Basque Country. A social and economic guide.
See item no. 23.

The Economic Agreement.
See item no. 223.

Industry and Trade

Early period

240 **Bilbao in the economy of the Basque Country and northwestern Europe during the Modern Era.**
Román Basurto. In: *Essays in Basque social anthropology and history.* Edited by William A. Douglass. Reno, Nevada: Basque Studies Program, University of Nevada, 1989, p. 215-34. (Basque Studies Program Occasional Papers Series, no. 4).

Basically a summary from Basurto's *Comercio y burguesía mercantil de Bilbao en la segunda mitad del siglo XVIII* (Bilbao, Spain: Universidad del País Vasco, 1983) (Trade and the merchant bourgoisie in XVIIIc. Bilbao), outlining Bilbao's fluctuating fortunes in the iron ore and wool trades and in fishing from the end of the Middle Ages to the early 18th century.

The art and tradition of the Zuloagas.
See item no. 327.

The French Region

241 **Activités en Pays Basque. Commerce, industrie, tourisme. Revue mensuelle.** (Activities in the Pays Basque. Commerce, industry, tourism. Monthly magazine.)
Bayonne, France: La Chambre de Commerce de Bayonne, 1950- . monthly.

An illustrated monthly magazine concentrating on business, especially tourism, in the French Basque region. In April 1990 it split to become *Activités en Pays Basque* (3 issues yearly) and *La Lettre d'activités en Pays Basque* (2 issues monthly). Subsequent frequency has varied.

The Spanish Region

242 **Bilbao's modern business élite.**
Eduardo J. Glas. Reno, Nevada: University of Nevada Press, 1997. 316p. maps. bibliog. (The Basque Series).

This recent study follows the development of the mining industry in the Bilbao region, and related economic expansion. Glas also examines the rise of the modern business class, in their cultural and social context, and the links between businesses and between the business world and politics.

243 **Catálogo de la industria navarra 1995.** (Industrial catalogue of Navarra 1995.)
Gobierno de Navarra, Sección de Estadística y Servicio de Industria. Pamplona, Spain: Gobierno de Navarra, Departamento de Industria, Comercio y Turismo, 1996. 238p.

An alphabetical listing of companies in Navarra with more than five employees, giving address, sales figures in pesetas, nature of business, products, materials used and trade marks. There are additional indexes by nature of business, listings of companies under municipality, and indexes of trade names and trade marks.

244 **Catálogo industrial de la Comunidad Autónoma Vasca.** (Industrial catalogue of the Basque Autonomous Community.)
Cámaras de Comercio de Alava, Bilbao & Guipúzcoa. Bilbao, Spain: Cámara de Comercio, Industria y Navegación de Bilbao, 1990. 2 vols.

The first part of this work lists companies with more than ten employees (with details of address, nature of business, trade names, number of employees), arranged alphabetically under province. The second volume lists companies according to the nature of their business, again under province.

245 **Cooperation at work. The Mondragon experience.**
Keith Bradley, Alan Gelb.   London: Heinemann Educational Books,
1983. 102p. bibliog.

After a brief historical introduction, this study focuses on industrial relations in the
Mondragón co-operatives. It compares their organization with conventional Western
firms, paternalistic Western models and Japanese companies. Mondragón's success is
explained in terms of its particular close-knit social environment and the co-operatives'
recruitment procedures.

246 **Directorio industrial del País Vasco.** (Industrial directory of the
Basque Country.)
Madrid: Instituto de la Pequeña y Mediana Empresa Industrial, 1992.
605p.

Firms are arranged by sector (energy, construction, etc.). Each entry includes address,
name of owner or managing director, nature of business, turnover, number of employees,
raw materials used, products and trade names. There are indexes of firms and products
and of firms listed by province and municipality.

247 **Euskal industria katalogoa = Catálogo industrial vasco.** (Basque
industrial catalogue.)
Gobierno Vasco, Departamento de Industria y Energía, Viceconsejería
de Administración y Planificación.   Vitoria-Gasteiz, Spain: Servicio
Central de Publicaciones del Gobierno Vasco, 1994. 2nd ed. 706p.

Consists of an alphabetical listing by company. It is a less easy to use at first than
other similar directories, because the principle activity and products are coded according
to the detailed system of NACE norms. There is also an index arranged by the area of
main activity. The English in the introduction is poor, but in the technical sections it is
excellent.

248 **Industri sektorearen kontuak = Cuentas del sector industrial,
1982- .** (Figures for the industrial sector, 1982- .)
Gobierno Vasco, Dirección de Estadística.   [Vitoria-Gasteiz, Spain]:
Eusko Jaurlaritza = Gobierno Vasco, [1985]- .

Lists firms by sector and by number of employees. Production figures are given for
each sector (energy, cement, glass, metal, food and drink, tobacco, textiles, leather,
wood, rubber, construction, machinery, automobiles, electrical goods). Issues since
1985 have been compiled and published by the Instituto Vasco de Estadística,
EUSTAT, with the title *Industri kontuak = Cuentas industriales* (Industrial accounts).

249 **Industrial democracy as process. Participatory action research in
the Fagor Cooperative Group of Mondragón.**
Davydd J. Greenwood, José Luis González.   Assen, the Netherlands:
Van Gorcum, 1992. 242p. bibliog. (Social science for social action:
toward organizational renewal, vol. 2).

The result of work by a professional social worker and anthropologist, and by members
of the Fagor Co-operative themselves. It analyses the past history and present culture

of the organization, and how it changes to meet circumstances. It also examines the conflicts that arise between the co-operative ethos and the directional imperatives found in conventional firms, and indicates possible methods of resolution.

250 Merkatal sektoreko kontuak = Cuentas del sector comercio, 86/88- . (Figures for the commercial sector, 86/88- .)
Instituto Vasco de Estadística. Vitoria-Gasteiz, Spain: EUSTAT, [1991]- .

Covers wholesale and retail trade in twenty-three areas of activity, in terms of number of employees, hours worked, profit margins, production figures, taxes and labour costs.

251 Mondragon. The Basque co-operatives.
A report of the Enquiry Delegation from the Royal Arsenal Co-operative Society Limited. [London]: the Society, [1979?]. 47p.

A brief, but interesting account of a representative sample of the co-operatives (including one run by and for women), written by members of the British co-operative movement.

252 Mondragon. An economic analysis.
Henk Thomas, Chris Logan. London: George Allen & Unwin, 1982. 218p. bibliog.

A detailed socio-economic analysis of the Mondragón co-operatives, covering the foundation and growth of the group, its historical context, and the role of the credit bank, Caja Laboral Popular. There are important chapters on job creation, education and training, economic performance, distribution of earnings and comparison with other labour-managed organizations.

253 The myth of Mondragón. Cooperatives, politics, and working-class life in a Basque town.
Sharryn Kasmir. Albany, New York: State University of New York, 1996. 243p. bibliog.

Explodes the idea that Mondragón represents a model of industrial democracy and worker participation through ownership. Previous studies are criticized for focusing on the views of managers, rather than workers. The latter do not feel that they are part of the decision-making process. The co-operative ideal is shown to have replaced trade unionism and worker activism with middle-class materialism and passivity. It is also shown not to be apolitical, as is often claimed, but linked to the conservative ideology of the Partido Nacionalista Vasco (Basque Nationalist Party).

254 The origins of modern industrialism in the Basque Country.
R. J. Harrison. Sheffield, England: Department of Economics and Social History, University of Sheffield, 1977. 18p. (Studies in Economic and Social History, no. 2).

An outline account of mining, shipbuilding and the iron and steel industries in the Spanish Basque region from the 1850s until 1918. The role of British interests and investment is highlighted, as are the increasing demands for protectionism from Basque industrialists during the first decade of this century.

255 **Ranking empresarial del País Vasco y Navarra: 1994.** (Business listing in the Basque Country and Navarra.)
Cámara Oficial de Comercio, Industria y Navegación de Bilbao.
Bilbao, Spain: La Cámara, 1994. 395p.
Covers 3,253 firms registered in Navarra and the Autonomous Community. They are ranked in terms of volume of sales, and the number of employees is also given. An index of the firms is included.

256 **Women workers in the Mondragon system of industrial cooperatives.**
Sally L. Hacker, Clara Elcorobairutia. *Gender & Society*, no. 1 (1987), p. 358-79.
A comparison of the situation of women in co-operatives with those in traditional capitalist firms shows that women (and men) benefit from greater job security in the former, and that women in co-operatives are less disdvantaged by wage differentials, compared with men in other organizations doing similar work. However, at the time of the study, women co-operative workers still found themselves at the bottom of the wage scale, felt excluded from management decisions, and were disdvantaged by increased professionalism in management and by greater reliance on new technologies.

257 **Worker-owners: the Mondragon achievement. The Caja Laboral Popular and the Mondragon co-operatives in the Basque Provinces of Spain.**
A report financed by the Anglo-German Foundation for the Study of Industrial Society and prepared by Alastair Campbell [et al.].
London; Bonn-Bad Godesberg, Germany: Anglo-German Foundation for the Study of Industrial Society, 1977. 69p.
A brief account of the foundation, history and theory of the Mondragón co-operatives and of the financial and co-ordinating role of the Caja Laboral. The possible application of the principles of Mondragón in Britain is also examined.

The Basque Country. A social and economic guide.
See item no. 23.

Basque Country.
See item no. 234.

The Basque Country: an industrial region.
See item no. 235.

Agriculture and Fishing

Early period

258   **Basque whaling in Labrador in the 16th century.**
Jean-Pierre Proulx, translated from the original French.   Ottawa: Environment Canada, Parks Service, National Historic Sites, 1993. 108p. map. bibliog.

In the mid-16th century the Basque whaling industry expanded into North American waters. Proulx's account describes the history of this venture, the whaling methods and technology employed and the economics of the industry in both the French and Spanish regions. The bibliography of this specialist topic is especially useful.

259   **Guipuzcoan shipping in 1571 with particular reference to the decline of the transatlantic fishing industry.**
Selma Huxley Barkham.   In: *Anglo-American contributions to Basque studies: essays in honor of Jon Bilbao.*   Edited by William A. Douglass, Richard W. Etulain, William H. Jacobsen Jr.   Reno, Nevada: Desert Research Institute, 1977, p. 73-81. (Desert Research Institute Publications on the Social Sciences, no. 13).

Drawing upon a recently discovered document in the Spanish Archivo General at Simancas, Barkham provides data for the numbers, tonnage and destinations of ships sailing out of ports in Gipuzkoa, distinguishes between cod and whaling vessels, and expands upon the names and activities of shipowners. The deep-sea cod and whaling industries were to suffer a dramatic decline as a result of the loss of trade with Flanders, royal levies of men, and the deployment of Basque ships on overseas exploration.

The Spanish Region

260   **1982ko Euskal Herriko K.A.ko nekazal Zentsua = Censo agrario 1982 de la C.A. de Euskadi.** (1982 Agricultural census of the Autonomous Community of Euskadi.)
Gobierno Vasco, Dirección de Estadística and Departamento de Agricultura y Pesca.   [Vitoria-Gasteiz, Spain]: Eusko Jaurlaritza = Gobierno Vasco, 1985. 3 vols.
Volumes two to three cover land use, livestock, machinery and labour force, while the first concentrates on data at a municipal level.

261   **The demise of agriculture in Fuenterrabia.**
Davydd J. Greenwood.   In: *The changing faces of rural Spain.*
Edited by Joseph B. Aceves, William A. Douglass.   Cambridge, Massachusetts; Schenkman Publishing Co.; New York; London: John Wiley, 1976, p. 29-44.
Summarizes his findings in *Unrewarding wealth*, item no. 264.

262   **Euskadiko K.A. nekazal zentsua = Censo agrario de la C.A. de Euskadi. 1989.** (Agricultural census of the Autonomous Community of Euskadi. 1989.)
Instituto Vasco de Estadística and Gobierno Vasco, Departamento de Agricultura y Pesca.   Vitoria-Gasteiz, Spain: EUSTAT, 1991. 4 vols.
Volumes two to four cover land use, livestock, machinery, labour force and profitability, while the first concentrates on information at a municipal level.

263   **Nekazal elikagai sektorearen estatistika urtekaria E.A.E. = Anuario estadístico del sector agroalimentario. C.A.P.V., 1988- .**
(Annual statistics of agriculture and food industries, 1988- .)
Gobierno Vasco, Departamento de Agricultura y Pesca.   Vitoria-Gasteiz, Spain: Eusko Jaurlaritzaren Argitalpen Zerbitzu Nagusia = Servicio Central de Publicaciones del Gobierno Vasco, 1989- .
Presents annual statistics covering the agriculture, fishing and food industries. The section on agriculture covers land use, yield and prices, and gives figures for the cattle and sheep industries and for forestry. Fishing data covers size and age of the fleet and size of catches. Food industry statistics give the number of factories, employees, hours worked and volume of production. Separate publications were issued for fishing (1986/87, 1988), agriculture (1986, 1987/88, 1989), and the food industry (1986/87, 1988).

264   **Unrewarding wealth. The commercialization and collapse of agriculture in a Spanish Basque town.**
Davydd J. Greenwood.   Cambridge, England: Cambridge University Press, 1976. 233p. 2 maps. bibliog.
Analyses the commercialization of farming and rural depopulation in the municipality of Fuenterrabia (Gipuzkoa) over the period 1920-69. In spite of rising prosperity resulting from tourism and industrialization, Basques left the land to take up urban occupations, which were often menial and lower paid. This apparent paradox is explained by the lowering of the social status of farming, and by the possibility of the preservation of independence and dignity in the expanding cities.

Baserria. (The Basque farmhouse.)
See item no. 186.

Echalar and Murelaga.
See item no. 189

Serving girls and sheepherders; emigration and continuity in a Spanish Basque village.
See item no. 194.

Transport and Communications

265 **De Vascongados a Euskotrenbideak (1906-1995).** (Basque railways [1906-95].)
Revista de los aficionados al tren maqueta y real, no. 3 (1995), 89p.
The narrow-gauge railways of the Basque Provinces are famous among enthusiasts, and still constitute an essential supplement to the main national network. This monographic issue is lavishly illustrated, and its brief chapters cover the history of the constituent companies, their routes, rolling stock and motive power, and present operations, which have been run by a public company since 1982.

266 **Euskadiko portuak = Puertos del País Vasco.** (Harbours of the Basque Country.)
Fernando Léonard, photographs by Mikel Arrazola. Vitoria-Gasteiz, Spain: Servicio Central de Publicaciones del País Vasco, 1991. 315p. maps. bibliog.
Describes thirteen harbours in the Basque Autonomous Community, excluding the major ports of Bilbao and Pasajes. The work combines brief descriptions and technical information on tides, breakwaters, quays and number and size of registered vessels with attractive colour photographs and maps. Texts of various laws (including that transferring responsibility for harbours to the Autonomous Community) and harbour regulations are appended. The text is in Spanish and Basque.

267 **Gipuzkoako trenak.** (Trains of Gipuzkoa.)
Juanjo Olaizola, photographs by José López. Donostia-San Sebastián, Spain: Gipuzkoako Foru Aldundia, Kultura eta Euskara Departamentua = Diputación Foral de Gipuzkoa, Departamento de Cultura y Euskara, 1995. 108p. bibliog. (Bertan, no. 10).
This study charts the rapid development of Gipuzkoa's local rail network between 1863 and 1926, and the completion in 1864 of the main broad-gauge line to the French border, via Donostia-San Sebastián. It also stresses the difficulties posed to railway

construction by the province's mountainous terrain. The photographs, some modern, others early, are impressive. As with other volumes in this series, an English translation of the Basque text is appended.

268 Narrow gauge rails through the *Cordillera*.
Mike Bent. [England]: Semaphore Press, 1998. 144p. maps. bibliog.

A most thorough scholarly study of the narrow-gauge network of northern Spain, and the only one in English. The author, a transport historian, draws on published and archival sources in Spain, and devotes over four chapters to the lines of the Basque Region, including a composite account of several journeys across the entire present-day network. He examines the development of industry and commerce, and relates this to the history of the railways of the various areas. He concludes with a full survey of the motive power on the public and industrial lines, drawing attention to the work of British builders. The book is generously illustrated with black-and-white photographs, many hitherto unpublished, and maps specially drawn by the author. Peter Allen and Robert Wheeler's earlier *Steam on the Sierra. The narrow gauge in Spain and Portugal* (London: Cleaver-Hume, 1960) devotes p. 25-48 to the Cantabrian coastal lines of which some twelve (including excellent photographs) deal with the Basque Region. Details are given of individual locomotives.

269 Vía estrecha en España. (Narrow gauge in Spain.)
Barcelona: MAF, 1994. 1 vol. (unpaginated).

The narrow-gauge lines of the Spanish Basque region figure prominently in this book, which consists almost entirely of photographs (the majority black-and-white), arranged by railway company. Translations of the captions are included.

Employment, Manpower and the Labour Movement

The French Region

270 **Structure de l'emploi et des professions au Pays Basque.** (Structure
of employment and the professions in the Pays Basque.)
Agence pour le Développement Economique du Pays Basque.
Bayonne, France: ADEPAB, 1994. 75 leaves. (Begira: Observatoire
Economique du Pays Basque, cahier 5).
Provides a breakdown of the population of the French Basque region in terms of
professionals, craftspersons, business persons, unskilled and semi-professional
employees, and unemployed and retired people. Comparative figures are given for the
surrounding region (Aquitaine), neighbouring provinces (Béarn and Landes), and for
the whole of France.

The Spanish Region

271 **They shall *not* pass. The autobiography of La Pasionaria.**
Dolores Ibarruri.   London: Lawrence & Wishart, 1966. 351p.
A translation of the autobiography of La Pasionaria, first published in Spanish as *El
único camino* (1962). Ibarruri was born into a mining family in Gallarta (Bizkaia) in
1895, and joined the socialist movement in Somorrostro. She became a Communist
and subsequently became the national leader of the Party. Her autobiography contains
recollections of her upbringing in Bizkaia, the miners' strike of 1903 and the background to industrial protest in the region. Robert Low's biography, *La Pasionaria: the
Spanish firebrand* (London: Hutchinson, 1992), draws on this material and adds
details of Ibarruri's unsatisfactory married life.

The Basques: the Franco years and beyond.
See item no. 209.

A rebellious people. Basques, protests, and politics.
See item no. 220.

Statistics

General

272 **Euroregión en cifras = Euroregioa zifratan = Eurorégion en chiffres.** (A Euroregion in figures.)
Instituto Vasco de Estadística. Vitoria-Gasteiz, Spain: EUSTAT, 1997. 11p.

A leaflet summarizing basic socio-economic statistics (population, employment, foreign trade, bank deposits, agriculture and fishing, industry, construction, trade, tourism, transport, education, health, environment) for Navarra, the Basque Autonomous Community and Aquitaine (containing the French Basque region), which together comprise a so-called Euroregion.

The French Region

273 **La France et ses régions. 1997.** (France and her regions. 1997.)
Institut National de la Statistique et des Études Economiques. Paris: INSEE, 1997. 226p. maps.

Contains statistics for the Aquitaine region (p. 20-22) covering population, employment, VAT receipts (for farming, fishing, services, industry) and a further series of demographic, social and economic statistics, arranged by region.

274 **Tableaux économiques de l'Aquitaine. 1996.** (Economic tables for Aquitaine. 1996.)
Institut National de la Statistique et des Études Economiques.
Bordeaux, France: INSEE Aquitaine, 1996. 196p. (Dossier no. 20).

This annual volume contains statistics for the department of Pyrénées Atlantiques, which includes the three French Basque Provinces and Béarn. Statistics cover all socio-economic aspects: population; environment; health; housing; education; employment; income; energy; agriculture; industry; construction; business; research and development; tourism; external trade; and administration.

The Spanish Region

275 **Euskal urtekari estatistikoa 1982- = Anuario estadístico vasco 1982- .** (Basque annual statistics, 1982- .)
Gobierno Vasco, Dirección de Estadística.   Vitoria-Gasteiz, Spain: Eusko Jaurlaritza = Gobierno Vasco, 1983- .

The edition for 1995 has sixteen sections, covering climate, population, employment, social security, health, education, culture, economy, agriculture and food, industry and energy, service industries, public administration, financial services, housing and buildings, justice and elections, plus two sections of statistical trends and tables. From the volume for 1986, compiled and published by the Instituto Vasco de Estadística (EUSTAT).

276 **Panorama 1994 Basque Country = Panorama 1994 [Pays Basque].**
Instituto Vasco de Estadística.   Vitoria-Gasteiz, Spain: EUSTAT, 1994. 107p. maps.

A useful statistical summary in English and French, covering environment, population, labour market, social services, culture, agriculture, industry, commerce, tourism, economy, transport, communications and the elections of 1990 and 1993.

277 **Panorama estadístico de Navarra 1990.** (Statistical panorama of Navarra 1990.)
Pamplona, Spain: Gobierno de Navarra, Departamento de Economía y Hacienda, 1991. 189p.

Contains basic statistics for Navarra for the period 1986-89, covering climate and geography, population, agriculture, industry, social services, transport, economy and finance.

278   **Udal-adierazleak 1994 = Indicadores municipales 1994.** (Municipal
indicators 1994.)
Instituto Vasco de Estadística.   [Vitoria-Gasteiz, Spain]: EUSTAT,
1994. 2 vols.

Provides basic statistical information on 247 town councils, covering population,
housing, industry, agriculture, education (including knowledge of Basque) and social
services. Although the work is intended for school students, it is of considerable potential
interest to researchers. There are two previous editions, published in 1986 and 1988.

Environment and Planning

279 **Euskadiko ingurugiroaren gauregungo egoaren laburpena = Resumen del estado actual del medio ambiente en Euskadi, 1986.** (Summary of the present state of the environment in Euskadi, 1986.) Gobierno Vasco, Viceconsejería de Medio Ambiente.   Vitoria-Gasteiz, Spain: Eusko Jaurlaritza, Lurralde Antolaketa eta Garraio Saila = Gobierno Vasco, Departamento de Política Territorial y Transportes, 1987. 372p. map.

Consists primarily of a series of statistical and analytical annexes in Spanish, covering water quality (underground, river and sea), effluents, air quality and noise pollution, preceded by a geographical introduction and policy statements by the Basque Government on the environment and environmental education.

Education, Science and Technology

280 **10 años de enseñanza bilingüe 1979-80; 1989-90.** (Ten years of bilingual education, 1979-80; 1989-90.)
Gobierno Vasco, Departamento de Educación, Universidades e Investigación. Vitoria-Gasteiz, Spain: Eusko Jaurlaritza Argitalpen Zerbitzu Nagusia = Servicio de Publicaciones del Gobierno Vasco, 1990. 140p. (Zabakunde lanak, no. 24).

An overview of the process of adaptation of the school system in the Autonomous Community to a bilingual framework. Three models of bilingual education are outlined: Basque as a foreign language; equal proportions; and predominantly Basque, with Spanish as an obligatory subject. Analysis is also included of efforts to improve both the competence of teachers to teach in Basque, and the standard of teaching materials.

281 **Ikerketa zientifikoko eta garapen teknologikoko iharduerei buruzko estatistika = Estadística sobre actividades en investigación científica y desarrollo tecnológico, 1990- .** (Research and development statistics, 1990- .)
Instituto Vasco de Estadística. Vitoria-Gasteiz, Spain: EUSTAT, 1992- .

Analyses funds and personnel involved in research and development in the private and public sectors and in higher education, by subject, source of funding and nature of occupation.

282   **Irakaskuntza-estatistika. Ikasle, irakasle eta irakaskuntza-zentruak = Estadística de la enseñanza. Alumnos, profesores y centros docentes, 82/83- .** (Education statistics. Pupils, teachers and teaching establishments, 1982/83- .)
Gobierno Vasco, Dirección de Estadística.   Vitoria-Gasteiz, Spain: Eusko Jaurlaritza = Gobierno Vasco, 1984- .

Provides annual statistics covering all types of education, including private, public and *ikastolak* (private Basque-language schools), and all levels from preschool to university, including adult and special education. Figures for bilingual (Spanish and Basque) and monolingual (Spanish or Basque) education are also given. Since 1984/85 the title has been *Irakaskuntzaren-estatistika = Estadística de la enseñanza* and the work is compiled and published by the Instituto Vasco de Estadística (EUSTAT).

Literature

General

283 **Le Basque et la littérature d'expression basque en Labourd,
Basse-Navarre et Soule.** (Basque and Basque literature in Labourd,
Basse Navarre and Soule.)
Pierre Lafitte.   Bayonne, France: Librairie Le Livre, 1941. 96p.
(Collection Aintzina).
The published version of a lecture given at the Musée Basque, Bayonne (3 April
1941). The author first describes the nature of the Basque language, and then
expounds the various theories concerning its origin, before briefly surveying the oral
literature of the *bertsolaris* and the popular theatre of the *pastorales* of Soule. The
remainder of the lecture consisted of a chronological survey of outstanding writers,
with brief biographical details and facts about their works. The final pages (p. 78-88)
contain an anthology of excerpts in French translation.

284 **Basque literature.**
Gorka Aulestia.   In: *Encyclopedia of world literature in the 20th
century.*   General editor: Leonard S. Klein.   New York: Ungar,
1981-84, rev. ed. vol. 2, p. 150-51, vol. 4, p. 310-11.
A very brief survey of modern Basque literature of both the French and Spanish
regions (regrettably placed under French and Spanish Literature respectively).
Aulestia emphasizes the predominance of religion in Basque letters until the 1960s,
and lists outstanding writers and their major works. A very basic bibliography for each
tradition is appended.

285 **The Basque poetic tradition.**
Gorka Aulestia.   Reno, Nevada: University of Nevada Press,
forthcoming. 248p. bibliog. (The Basque Series).

An introduction to the history of poetry in Basque, from Bernard Etxepare (1545), the
first poet whose work was printed, down to contemporary writers. Aulestia also
studies *bertsolaritza* (i.e. popular oral verse) and the pioneering works of prominent
19th- and 20th-century poets. He analyses both the native themes and traditional elements of Basque poetry, as well as poetic forms adopted from poetry in other
European languages.

286 **A comparative study of Basque and Yugoslav troubadourism.**
Gorka Aulestia.   *World Literature Today*, vol. 59, no. 3 (1985),
p. 382-85.

Aulestia compares Basque *bertsolaritza* with the Serbo-Croatian oral epic poetry
studied by Milman Parry and Albert B. Lord, and concludes that the Basque poets rely
more heavily upon improvisation, as there are no traditional topics or themes, and that
memory, rather than the use of formulae, plays an important role in composition.

287 **Congreso de literatura. Hacia la literatura vasca.** (Conference on
literature. An approach to Basque literature.)
II. Euskal Mundu Biltzarra = II Congreso Mundial Vasco.   Madrid:
Castalia, 1989. 589p.

Contains the papers, all in Spanish, presented at the Conference on Literature (Vitoria-
Gasteiz, 1987) as part of the Second World Basque Congress. Twelve deal with literature
in Basque from ballads and *bertsolaritza* to contemporary poetry and fiction. The
remainder cover literary theory or literature in Spanish, some by writers of Basque origin.

288 **Double minorities of Spain. A bio-bibliographic guide to women
writers of the Catalan, Galician and Basque countries.**
Edited by Kathleen McNerney, Cristina Enríquez de Salamanca.   New
York: Modern Language Association of America, 1994. 421p.

Contains entries for twenty Basque writers, alongside 421 Catalans and 31 Galicians.
Each article consists of a brief biography, a description of the writer's work, lists of
books and articles, works translated into Spanish or English, and critical studies of the
author. Besides well-known Basque writers such as Arantxa Urretavizcaya, obscure
figures such as Patxika Erramuzpe (a 20th-century poet) are included. Strangely,
Vicenta Moguel (1782-1854) is omitted. There is no index by nationality.

289 **Historia de la literatura vasca.** (History of Basque literature.)
Luis Michelena.   Madrid: Ediciones Minotauro, 1960. 180p. bibliog.
(Biblioteca vasca, no. 7).

An extremely readable literary history that concentrates upon the oral tradition and on
major works down to 1850. Michelena, like other historians of Basque literature,
includes translations into Basque and works on the language, and his approach is culturally broad, setting Basque in a wider European context. The treatment of the period
after 1850 is slighter. The bibliography is full, although the later period again receives
less attention.

290 **Historia de la literatura vasca.** (History of Basque literature.)
Luis Villasante. Oñate, Spain: Aranzazu, 1979. 2nd ed. 487p.

A very solid and reliable history of Basque literature in its widest sense, taking in translations of the Bible and other religious texts, and the work of linguists, including non-Basques such as Edward Spencer Dodgson and Victor Stempf. The work is organized chronologically, with separate sections on each writer. It was first published in 1961, and the second edition briefly covers the ensuing period until ca. 1975. It is strongest on biographical and bibliographical information.

291 **Historia social de la literatura vasca.** (Social history of Basque literature.)
Ibon Sarasola, translated by Jesús Antonio Cid. Madrid: Akal, 1976. 183p. (Akal 74).

Covers the same period as Villasante (item no. 290), but Sarasola places more emphasis on aspects of language and the absence of a standard written form of Basque. He also devotes more attention to broader intellectual and cultural movements. The first three parts form a chronological account, while the fourth and last ('writers and works') is a mine of useful information. Sarasola's critical judgements offer the non-specialist a starting point. The book was originally published in Basque in 1971.

292 **Improvisational poetry from the Basque Country.**
Gorka Aulestia. Reno, Nevada: University of Nevada Press, 1987. 252p. bibliog.

Bertsolaritza is the orally composed poetry of the Basques, which has thrived continuously for the past two centuries, but whose long-lost origins go back considerably further. Aulestia's thorough survey covers its history, comparisons with similar poetry in other languages, the nature of the verse itself (its forms, themes and language) and the work of individual poets. The many quotations are in the original Basque with English translation. The book was first published in Spanish entitled *Bertsolarismo* (Bilbao, Spain: Bizkaiko Foru Aldundia, 1990).

293 **Literatura vasca.** (Basque literature.)
Jon Juaristi. Madrid: Taurus, 1987. 161p. bibliog. (Historia crítica de la literatura hispánica, no. 29).

A useful complement to both Villasante and Sarasola (item nos. 290 and 291), especially as it covers the period since the mid-1970s. Juaristi emphasizes specifically literary aspects and the history of ideas. He also charts the full emergence of literature, post-1975, from the religious and political preoccupations of earlier generations of writers.

294 **Poetry and politics: Basque poetry as an instrument of national revival.**
Gorka Aulestia. *World Literature Today*, vol. 55, no. 1 (1981), p. 48-52; vol. 56, no. 3 (1982), p. 457-61.

A survey of 19th- and 20th-century Basque poetry from both the French and Spanish regions, seen as an expression of national identity and of protest against oppression. Religious writers dominated Basque literature as recently as the middle of this century, and Aulestia charts the emergence of completely secular poetry since the

1960s. This is one of the very few studies of Basque literature in English. The quotations are in Basque with English translation.

A book of the Basques.
See item no. 6.

Singing duels and social solidarity: the case of the Basque *Charivari*.
See item no. 362.

Translations into English

295 **Contemporary Basque fiction. An anthology, introduction and commentary.**
Jesús María Lasagabaster, translated by Michael E. Morris.   Reno, Nevada; Las Vegas: University of Nevada Press, 1990. 95p. (The Basque Series).
Consists of ten short stories, or excerpts from novels, by established Basque writers, including Txillardegi, Bernardo Atxaga, Anjel Lertxundi, Ramón Saizarbitoria and Arantxa Urretavizcaya. The introduction (p. 1-23) charts the break with the prevailing tradition of *costumbrismo* (descriptions of local types and customs), the influences operating upon contemporary Basque novelists, and current trends. There are brief biographies of each writer. The book was first published in Spanish in 1986 (Barcelona, Spain: Edicions del Mall). The original Basque has apparently been translated directly into English.

296 **Linguae vasconum primitiae.** (The first fruits of the Basque language.)
Bernard Etxepare.   Bilbao, Spain: Real Academia de la Lengua Vasca = Euskaltzaindia, 1995. 409p. 2 maps.
An anniversary edition, with translations into five modern European languages (Spanish, English, French, German and Italian), of the first book to be printed in Basque (Bordeaux, 1545), consisting of poems on religion, love, freedom and the Basque language. The author, Etxepare (Echepare or Dechepare – the spelling varies), was parish priest at St.-Michel-le-Vieux near St.-Jean-Pied-de-Port (Basse Navarre). The brief introduction (in Basque and translated into all five languages) covers the poet's life and examines his poetry. The text of the only surviving copy of the first edition, now in the Bibliothèque Nationale, Paris, is reproduced in facsimile.

297 **The lone man.**
Bernardo Atxaga, translated from the Spanish by Margaret Jull Costa. London: Harvill Press, 1996. 320p.
An English translation of *El hombre solo* (1994), the Spanish version of Atxaga's *Gizona bere bakardadean* (also 1994). It tells the story of Carlos, a former ETA

activist, now running a hotel outside Barcelona, who has agreed to conceal two escaped gunmen. The police are in his hotel to protect the Polish football team during the World Cup, but Carlos realizes that he must get the gunmen away.

298 **Obabakoak. A novel.**
Bernardo Atxaga, translated by Margaret Jull Costa. London: Hutchinson, 1992. 326p.

Bernardo Atxaga (b. 1951) is probably the most celebrated novelist writing in Basque today. His novel about 'events that happened in Obaba' (an imaginary Basque village) has been translated into several European languages. It consists of a series of seemingly unrelated tales that achieve a thematic unity. The translation is based on Atxaga's own Spanish version (1989) of the Basque original (1988).

Translations into Spanish and French

299 **Allende el viento.** (Beyond the wind.)
Txillardegi. Donostia, Spain: Haranburu, 1984. 179p.

A translation of *Haizeaz bestaldetik* (1979) by José Luis Álvarez Enparantza (b. 1929), who uses the pen name Txillardegi. This is a difficult novel, more poetic prose than narrative, in which the wind and sea, so much a feature of the Basque landscape, play a large part. Txillardegi was at one time a member of ETA, and was forced to live in France.

300 **Cien metros.** (One hundred metres.)
Ramón Saizarbitoria. Madrid: Nuestra Cultura, 1979. 105p.
(Colección Pueblos ibéricos, 11; Serie Euskadi).

Published in 1976 in Basque under the title of *Ehun metro*, Saizarbitoria's novel incurred the initial displeasure of the Juzgado de Orden Público (Public Order Court). It narrates the last thoughts of a Basque terrorist as he recalls his life. 'One hundred metres' refers to the fugitive's last few yards as the police close in. The novel was technically innovative in using more than one narrative voice, and, in the original, in its mixture of Basque narrative and Spanish dialogue. A more recent edition has appeared: Hernani, Spain: Orain, 1995 (Egin Biblioteka).

301 **Cuentos nocturnos.** (Tales of the night.)
Mario Onaindia. Barcelona, Spain: Edhasa, 1991. 115p.

A collection of five short stories, translated by the author himself from the Basque original, entitled *Gau ipuinak*. Onaindia is equally well known as a politician. He was condemned to death at the Burgos trial of 1968 (his sentence was commuted) and subsequently became a member of the Spanish Socialist Party.

302 **Dos hermanos. El cuarto canto.** (Two brothers. The fourth canto.)
Bernardo Atxaga. Madrid: Ollero & Ramos, 1995. 157p. (Novelas ejemplares).

This is Atxaga's own Spanish version of his short novel *Bi anai* (originally published in 1985). Through the eyes of various birds and animals, it tells the unfortunate story of two young brothers in Obaba, Atxaga's imaginary village, one of whom falls hopelessly in love.

303 **Esos cielos.** (Those skies.)
Bernardo Atxaga. Barcelona, Spain: Ediciones B, 1996. 142p. (Ficcionario).

A short novel, the action of which takes place during a bus journey from Barcelona to Bilbao, as Irene, just released from prison for a terrorism-related offence, travels back to her home city. The story consists of her recollections of her stay in prison, and of her encounters with her fellow passengers, including two policemen who seek her collaboration, and two nuns. An English translation, entitled *The lone woman,* has been announced by Harvill Press for early 1999.

304 **Euskal baladen lorea = Flor de baladas vascas.** (Flowering of Basque ballads.)
Edited by Jon Juaristi. Madrid: Visor, 1989. 183p. bibliog. (Colección Visor de poesía, no. 239).

An anthology of ballads, in Basque with parallel Spanish translation, preceded by a brief introduction in Spanish. The poems are grouped in five sections: early fragments (from the 14th to the 16th centuries, but preserved in late 16th- and early 17th-century chronicles); ballads linked to noble Pyrenean families; ballads in the pan-European tradition; children's ballads; and 19th- and 20th-century compositions in traditional form.

305 **Memorias de una vaca.** (Recollections of a cow.)
Bernardo Atxaga. Madrid: Ediciones SM, 1992. 206p. (El Barco de vapor. Serie Oro).

A Spanish translation of Atxaga's hugely successful novel *Behi euskaldun baten memoriak* (Pamplona, 1992). It consists of imaginary dialogues between a cow, Mo, and her friend, and between Mo and her inner voice. Unlike most of his other novels, Atxaga did not himself translate it.

306 **Oraiko olerki sorta-bat = Anthologie poésie basque contemporaine.** (Anthology of Basque contemporary poetry.)
Bayonne, France: Centre Culturel du Pays Basque, 1988. 305p.

A collection of 20th-century Basque poetry, in Basque with parallel French translation.

307 **Los pasos incontables.** (So many steps.)
Ramón Saizarbitoria.   Madrid: Espasa-Calpe, 1998. 368p. (Espasa Narrativa).

A Basque novelist fights against the fallibility of memory in his endeavour to reconstruct the last days of a man condemned to death in 1975, right at the end of the Franco régime. The translation is by the essayist and literary critic Jon Juaristi.

308 **Peru Abarka.**
Juan Antonio de Moguel, bilingual edition by Resurrección M.ª Azkue, translated by Juan Carlos Cortázar.   Bilbao, Spain: La Gran Enciclopedia Vasca, 1970. 2nd ed. 157p. (Separatas de la Gran Enciclopedia Vasca, no. 4).

Juan Antonio de Moguel (1745-1804) composed one of the classics of Basque literature, a series of dialogues between a farmer and a barber intended to illustrate correct Basque usage, which he considered to be that of rural speakers in 18th-century Bizkaia. The original work, entitled *El doctor Peru Abarca, catedrático de la Universidad de Basarte o Diálogo entre un rústico solitario bascongado y un barbero callejero llamado Maisu Juan* (Doctor Peru Abarca, Professor of the University of Basarte or Dialogue between a solitary Basque peasant and a street barber called Maisu Juan), was published in 1881.

309 **¿Por qué Panpox?** (Why, my pet?)
Arantxa Urretabizkaia.   Hernani, Spain: Orain, 1995. 94p. (Egin biblioteka).

Urretabizkaia's first novel, *Zergatik Panpox?* (1979), appears in Spanish translation, together with a collection of her early poetry. The novel consists of a monologue, addressed by a woman to her little son, concerning their life with the boy's father, who has just left them.

310 **Proverbes et poésies basques.** (Basque proverbs and poems.)
Arnaud d'Oyhénart, trilingual edition (Basque-French-Spanish), introduction and notes by Jean-Baptiste Orpustan, Spanish translation by Fermintxo Arkotxa.   St. Étienne de Baïgorry, France: Izpegi, 1992. 283p. (Collection 'Lettres').

Arnaud d'Oyhénart (1592-1667), having studied law at Bordeaux, became a deputy for Soule (1623-29). He subsequently acted as a lawyer on behalf of the Parliament of Basse Navarre. He wrote a history of the Basques in Latin, *Notitia utriusque Vasconiae* ('Concerning the two Basque Regions', 1638), and in 1657 he published a book containing his poetry and a collection of 706 Basque proverbs, together with his own French translation and a Basque-French glossary of difficult words. Orpustan's most valuable edition contains all of Oyhénart's text, including his French prefaces to the poems and the proverbs, René Lafon's prose translation of the *Poésies* and a Spanish version of the whole. Lafon's 1955 article, 'Notes pour une édition critique et une traduction française des poésies d'Oyhénart' (Notes for a critical edition and French translation of Oyhénart's poetry), is reprinted as an appendix.

311   **Santa Grazi: pastorala.** (Sainte-Engrâce: *pastorale.*)
      Junes Casenave.   Arantzazu-Oiñati, Spain: Jakin, 1976. 175p.
The Basque *pastorales* of Sainte-Engrâce, in the dialect of Soule, are the most famous examples of Basque popular theatre. The introduction to this edition is in Basque, but the original text is accompanied by a French translation.

312   **Saturno.** (Saturn.)
      Arantxa Urretabizkaia, translated by Maite González Esnal, Arantxa
      Urretabizkaia.   Madrid: Alfaguara, 1989. 137p. (Alfaguara Hispánica,
      no. 59).
The Spanish translation appeared two years after the Basque original of Urretabizkaia's novel about a sailor's relationship with a woman whom he identifies with the planet Saturn.

313   **Las últimas sombras (Otto Pette).** (The last shadows. [Otto Pette].)
      Anjel Lertxundi, translated by Jorge Giménez Bech.   Barcelona,
      Spain: Seix Barral, 1996. 316p.
Spanish translation of the novel *Otto Pette* (published in 1994) by Lertxundi (b. 1948), which demonstrated the strength of Basque contemporary fiction. Rather than taking as its theme Basque history or politics, it tells of a medieval nobleman who is obliged to question the existing social order by a mysterious stranger who arrives unannounced at his house.

The Arts

Visual arts

314   **Arte vasco.** (Basque art.)
      Jesús Altuna [et al.], introduction by Juan Plazaola.   San Sebastián,
      Spain: Erein, 1982. 269p.
A collection of articles focusing on the visual arts and architecture of the Basque
region from prehistoric times to the present. It is neither a chronological exposition
nor a definition of Basque art.

315   **Arte vasco.** (Basque art.)
      Bilbao, Spain: Bilboarte, 1994. 333p.
An introduction to the work of forty contemporary Spanish Basque painters, all
figurative, with the vast majority being little known outside the region. The entry for
each artist consists of a brief appreciation, including his or her medium, themes and
style, together with full-page colour reproductions of examples of their work.

316   **Artistas vascos.** (Basque artists.)
      Bilbao, Spain: Bilboarte, 1994. 481p.
Despite the seemingly identical publication date, this is a subsequent volume to item
no. 315. The format and editorial criteria are similar. Another group of artists is
introduced, but more space is devoted to drawing and sculpture.

317 **Catálogo de la exposición de pintura de Ignacio Zuloaga, 1870-1945 = Ignacio Zuloagaren 1870-1945 pintura-erakusketaren katalogoa.** (Catalogue of the exhibition of paintings by Ignacio Zuloaga, 1870-1945.)
Vitoria-Gasteiz, Spain: Eusko Jaurlaritza, Kultura eta Turismo Saila, 1985. 151p. bibliog.

A bilingual Basque and Spanish catalogue of an exhibition of Zuloaga's work held at the Museo de San Telmo, San Sebastián (November 1985-January 1986), consisting of seventy-eight works representative of all periods of the artist's career. There are introductory essays on his career and work by Enrique Lafuente Ferrari and Julián Gallego. The most noteworthy feature, however, is the extensive, chronological bibliography (p. 83-140). Relatively few of the works that were exhibited are reproduced.

318 **Chillida.**
London: South Bank Centre, 1990. 128p. bibliog.

A catalogue of the exhibition held at the Hayward Gallery, London (6 September-4 November 1990), of Chillida's smaller sculptures and drawings. Three critical essays are included, together with an interview with the sculptor. Many of the exhibits are reproduced, and there are also photographs of Chillida's monumental sculptures in the Spanish Basque region and at Gijón.

319 **Chillida at Gernika. Birth of a monument: 'Gure aitaren etxea' = 'Our father's house'.**
J. M. Tasende. La Jolla, California: Tasende Gallery, 1988. unpaginated.

A catalogue of a touring exhibition in the United States designed to coincide with the installation of Eduardo Chillida's monumental concrete sculpture at Gernika (Bizkaia), marking the fiftieth anniversary of the destruction of the town in 1937, during the Spanish Civil War. There are brief essays by Thomas M. Messer on Chillida, and by Robert Laxalt on Gernika's symbolic significance.

320 **Chillida. Two public spaces in the Basque Country.**
Photographs by F. Catalá Roca, J. Mezzacala, Jon Llanos.
Vitoria-Gasteiz, Spain: Basque Government, Culture Department, 1985. unpaginated.

A collection of black-and-white photographs of Eduardo Chillida's *Peine de los vientos* (Wind combs) at San Sebastián, and of his monument to the Defence of the Fueros in the old market square (Plaza de Abastos) in Vitoria. Both works were collaborations with the architect Luis Peña Ganchegui.

321 **Darío de Regoyos.**
Donostia-San Sebastián, Spain: Kutxa Fundazioa = Fundación Social y Cultural de la Caja Gipuzkoa-San Sebastián, 1994. 421p. bibliog. (Antologías Kutxa, no. 52).

A catalogue of an exhibition entitled 'Regoyos y el País Vasco', held in San Sebastián, July-September 1994. Regoyos (1857-1912) was born in Ribadesella

(Asturias), but from 1871 he was raised and educated in Madrid. He settled in Irún in 1882, moving to San Sebastián in 1890. Famous primarily as a landscape artist, he painted many views of the Basque region, a number of which are reproduced in this catalogue, together with some portraits and drawings. The extensive introduction, in Spanish and Basque, deals in detail with Regoyos's life, artistic career and his relations with writers and other painters.

322 **Diccionario de pintores vascos.** (Dictionary of Basque painters.)
Mario Angel Marrodán. Madrid: Beramar, 1989. 5 vols.

An alphabetically arranged, collective biography of some 10,000 artists born, or residing, in the Basque Region. The information covers studies, prizes, exhibitions, location of works and chosen medium. There is little historical or critical commentary.

323 **Escultores vascos. Oteiza, Basterretxea, Ugarte.** (Basque sculptors.)
Oviedo, Spain: Caja de Ahorros de Asturias, 1991. 121p. bibliog.

An exhibition catalogue, well supplied with black-and-white photographs, illustrating the work of three notable Basque sculptors.

324 **Gure artea 1996.** (Our art 1996.)
Gobierno Vasco, Departamento de Cultura. Vitoria-Gasteiz, Spain: Eusko Jaurlaritza, Argitalpen Zerbitzu Nagusia = Servicio Central de Publicaciones, Gobierno Vasco, 1996. 72p.

An illustrated publication containing commentaries and technical information in Basque and Spanish devoted to contemporary art by Spanish Basque artists.

325 **The life and work of Ignacio Zuloaga.**
Enrique Lafuente Ferrari. Barcelona, Spain: Planeta, 1991. 593p. bibliog.

An English translation of the third edition of Lafuente Ferrari's work, first published in Spanish in 1972. Zuloaga (1870-1945) achieved fame, and some notoriety, outside the Basque region. Only a small proportion of his output represents Basque scenes and characters. The first part of the book deals in detail with the artists's life, the second with his aesthetic ideas, the periods of his career, his landcapes and his portraits. A listing of his paintings is included but it is incomplete for the early and later periods of his life.

326 **Tesoros del Museo de Bellas Artes de Bilbao. Pintura, 1400-1939.**
(Treasures of the Museum of Fine Art, Bilbao. Painting, 1400-1939.)
Edited by Juan J. Luna. Madrid: Fundación Rich, 1989. 207p. bibliog.

A catalogue of an exhibition held at the Museo Municipal, Madrid (November 1989-January 1990). The catalogue reproduces a small sample of paintings by Basque artists, including Ignacio Zuloaga and Ramón and Valentín de Zubiaurre. The works include landscapes, portraits and scenes of Basque life, the latter being examples of the distinctive 'Basque' school of the late 19th and early 20th century.

Decorative arts

327 **The art and tradition of the Zuloagas. Spanish damascene from the Khalili collection.**
James D. Lavin, with an essay by Ramiro Larrañaga. [London?]: Khalili Family Trust in association with the Victoria and Albert Museum, 1997. 261p. map.

A catalogue of an exhibition of the decorative metalwork of Plácido Zuloaga, held at the Victoria and Albert Museum in London in 1997-98. The Zuloaga family were distinguished armourers who had worked both in Madrid and at Eibar (Gipuzkoa). Plácido was responsible for transforming his father's gun factory at Eibar, in the mid-19th century, into one forging art objects that achieved fame across Europe, particularly in England. The catalogue is lavishly illustrated and contains scholarly essays on damascening in Spain (Lavin), damascening and engraving (Larrañaga) and on the Zuloagas (Lavin). Plácido's son was the painter Ignacio (see item no. 325).

328 **Cerámica popular vasca.** (Traditional Basque pottery.)
Enrike Ibabe Ortiz. Bilbao, Spain: Fundación Bilbao Bizkaia Kutxa, 1995. 290p.

A well-illustrated survey of regional pottery produced since the middle of the last century in the Spanish Basque region, arranged by place of manufacture. Technical details are given covering type of clay and glaze, specifications of wheels and ovens, and methods of manufacture.

329 **Le mobilier basque. Ensemble & détails.** (Basque furniture. An overview.)
Louis Colas. Paris: Ch. Massin, c. 1920. 9p. 40 plates. (Collection de l'art régional en France).

The introduction describes very briefly the simple forms of Basque decoration. The large plates, however, give a good idea of the French Basque region's massive style of furniture.

Architecture

330 **Catálogo monumental de Navarra.** (Catalogue of the monuments of Navarra.)
Directed by María Concepción García Gainza. Pamplona, Spain: Institución Príncipe de Viana, 1982-97. 8 vols. maps.

A truly monumental work, which describes both civil and religious buildings (and the paintings, sculpture and other art works that they contain), and examples of vernacular architecture found throughout the five *merindades* of Navarra (Tudela, Estella, Olite, Sangüesa and Pamplona). Within each volume the material is arranged alphabetically by place-name. Each entry gives brief historical descriptions of the noteworthy buildings, plus information about their location and ground plans. There are many black-and-white and some colour photographs.

331   **Gipuzkoako dorretxeak eta leinuak.** (Towers and lineages of Gipuzkoa.)
F. Borja de Aguinagalde, photographs by José Luis Galiana.
Donostia-San Sebastián, Spain: Gipuzkoako Foru Aldundia, Kultura eta Euskara Departamentua = Diputación Foral de Gipuzkoa, Departamento de Cultura y Euskara, 1997. 107p. bibliog. (Bertan, no. 11).

The tower is a distinctive feature of the society and landscape of medieval Gipuzkoa, being the form of the frequently fortified manor house inhabited by the local ruling noble family. They served not just a political role, but also a socio-economic one, as the focal point of both rural and urban economies. The text looks at the function of the towers in both contexts, and at the varied architectural features that they display. Like the other volumes in this series, this one has numerous colour photographs, and the English translation (which is poor) of the Basque original is appended.

332   **Navarre romane.** (Romanesque Navarra.)
Luis María de Lojendio, English translation by David Rowe, Paul Veyriras.   St.-Léger-de-Vauban, France: Zodiaque, 1967. 399p. map. bibliog. (La Nuit des temps, no. 26).

A similar format is followed in this guide to the Romanesque architecture of Navarra as in item no. 334. It concentrates on the abbey church of Leyre, the churches of Santa María at Ujué and Sangüesa, San Pedro de Aibar, San Martín de Artaiz and Pamplona cathedral. An English summary is appended.

333   **Pays Basque roman: Álava, Biscaya, Gipúzcoa.** (Romanesque in the Basque Country: Alava, Bizkaia, Gipuzkoa.)
José Javier López de Ocáriz.   St.-Léger-de-Vauban, France: Zodiaque, 1997. 334p. map. bibliog. (La Nuit des temps, no. 87).

A detailed guide to the Romanesque architecture of the three Spanish Basque Provinces, concentrating on seven principal buildings, with additional material on smaller and late-Romanesque churches, and statues of the Virgin Mary. The main sections include ground plans, dimensions, building history and a commentary on the architectural features of each monument. There are many black-and-white and colour photographs. Unlike earlier volumes in this series (item nos. 332 and 334), this one has no English summary.

334   **Pyrénées romanes.** (Romanesque in the Pyrenees.)
Marcel Durliat, Victor Allégre, English translation by P. Fontaney.
St.-Léger-de-Vauban, France: Zodiaque, 1969. 374p. 4 maps. bibliog. (La Nuit des temps, no. 30).

A guide to Romanesque architecture similar to item no. 332, but covering the small number of Romanesque monuments in the French Basque region, notably the collegiate church of Sainte-Engrâce and the hospital of Saint-Blaise (Soule). An English summary is appended.

Historic and monumental guide of Gipuzkoa.
See item no. 61.

Baserria.
See item no. 186.

Music and dance

335 Basque dance.
John M. Ysursa.   Boise, Idaho: Tamarack Books, 1995. 108p. 2 maps. bibliog.
The author was Dance Director of the Boise Oinkari Basque Dancers (Idaho) for five years, and his book focuses on the dance tradition familiar to the Basque American communities of east Oregon and south Idaho. He describes the nature of the dances of the provinces of Gipuzkoa, Navarra and in particular those of Bizkaia, the ancestral home of the majority of Idaho Basques. Another chapter is devoted to the dances associated with Carnival in the Basque Region. An important element of his study is his consideration of a possible symbolic, pre-Christian meaning in many of the dances.

336 Basque music.
J. A. Arana Martija.   Donostia-San Sebastián, Spain: Erein, sponsored by the Basque Government, 1985. 93p.
An illustrated overview of music in the Basque region from earliest times to the present. There are sections on folk and religious music, organ builders, and individual composers, including Joannes Antxieta, Juan Crisóstomo Arriaga, Maurice Ravel and Jesús Guridi, concluding with paragraphs on contemporary musical life (performers, musical education and composers).

337 Dances of France III: the Pyrenees.
Violet Alford.   London: Max Parrish, 1952. 38p.
Alford devotes just two pages (15-17) to the dances of the Basque region, including the fandango, a version of the Aragonese *jota*; the string dance; the *saut basque*; and the sword dance transplanted from Bizkaia, which she saw as detrimental to the local tradition.

338 Danzas de Euskalerri. (Dances of the Basque Country.)
Gaizka de Barandiarán.   San Sebastián, Spain: Auñamendi, 1963. 3 vols. (Colección Auñamendi, 30-31, 67-68).
A very detailed, highly technical, choreographic and structural analysis of Basque popular dances, accompanied by line drawings and musical illustrations.

339 **Música vasca.** (Basque music.)
José Antonio Arana Martija. Bilbao, Spain: Caja de Ahorros
Vizcaína, 1987. 2nd ed. 424p. (Biblioteca musical del País Vasco,
no. 1).
Covers much the same material as item no. 336, but in greatly expanded form, and in
Spanish. The final section addresses the question of whether it is possible to speak of
'Basque music', and what its characteristics might be.

340 **Regional dances of Europe. A guide to background and
presentation. Regions: Basque; Portugal; Northern Spain; Turkey;
Italy; Finland.**
Helen Wingrave, Robert Harrold. London: Published by the authors,
1970. 44p.
Contains a brief, but very useful introduction to the music, steps and associated
customs of Basque popular dance. The steps and music of three dances (a fandango, a
progressive group dance and a Basque solo dance) are given.

341 **Sword dance and drama.**
Violet Alford. London: Merlin Press, 1962. 222p.
Although the Spanish Basques themselves see their sword dances as primarily war
dances (p. 165-70), they are in reality, according to the author, a form of pan-
European chain dance, with a variety of symbolic meanings relating to the seasons,
fertility, death and resurrection, etc. She describes examples from Navarra, Gipuzkoa
and Bizkaia.

342 **The traditional dance.**
Violet Alford, Rodney Gallop. London: Methuen, 1933. 204p.
Chapter 9, 'Religious dances', describes the sword dances of Oñate (Gipuzkoa) and
Lesaca (Navarra), both performed in church, as well as religious dances from
Arbéroue (Basse Navarre) and Lequeitio (Bizkaia).

Pyrenean festivals.
See item no. 360.

Cinema

343 **El cine y los vascos.** (The Basques and the cinema.)
José María Unsain. San Sebastián, Spain: Eusko-Ikaskuntza, 1985.
355p. (Cuadernos de sección; Cinematografía, no. 1).
A comprehensive treatment of cinema and film in the Spanish Basque region. The
author studies the making of films, the contributions of Basques to cinema, Basque
writers (e.g. Pío Baroja and Miguel de Unamuno) and their attitudes to film, and the
history of cinema clubs and festivals. A brief section on television is also included.

344   **Euskal zinema 1981-1989 = Cine vasco 1981-1989 = Basque cinema 1981-1989.**
Euskadiko Filmategia = Filmoteca Vasca.   Vitoria-Gasteiz, Spain: Eusko Jaurlaritza, Kultura eta Turismo Saila = Gobierno Vasco, Departamento de Cultura y Turismo, 1990. 167p.

A catalogue of feature films and shorts produced in the Basque Autonomous Community. Brief plot summaries are given in Basque, French and English, illustrated with stills in colour and reproductions of posters. Essential credits are listed. The text of the decree setting up the public company Euskofilm is also included. Virtually all the feature films are about Basques, are set in the Basque region, or are on Basque themes. Some are versions of novels included in this bibliography (*Ehun metro*, item no. 300, *Zergatik Panpox*, item no. 309), or are on recurrent themes: terrorism; witchcraft; Carlism; and rural emigration.

345   **San Sebastián: un festival, una historia (1953-1966).** (San Sebastián: a festival and its history [1953-66].)
José Luis Tuduri.   San Sebastián, Spain: Filmoteca Vasca = Euskadiko Filmategia, 1989. 303p.

An illustrated history of the San Sebastián international film festival from its inception in 1953 until the fourteenth festival in 1966. There are two indexes of film titles, one in the original language and the other in Spanish. The author is a film critic.

Cuisine

346   **Cuisine basque et béarnaise.** (Recipes from the Basque Country and Béarn.)
Michel Barberousse.   Biarritz, France: [Published by the author], 1964[?]. 108p.

A collection of unpretentiously presented recipes from the French Basque region and Béarn, embracing a wide range of dishes and desserts.

347   **Diccionario enciclopedia de gastronomía vasca.** (Encyclopaedic dictionary of Basque gastronomy.)
Iñaki Arrien [et al.].   Donostia-San Sebastián, Spain: Cofradía Vasca de Gastronomía, 1992. 968p.

A detailed and comprehensive reference work, containing approximately 7,000 entries relating to eating, drinking and cooking in the Basque region. Headwords are in Spanish, together with their Basque equivalents, and dialectal variants are included. Birds, fish and vegetables are also given in their Latin forms. Recipes are given which are associated with particular ingredients.

348 **Life and food in the Basque Country.**
María José Sevilla.   London: Weidenfeld & Nicolson, 1989. 170p.
Consists of a series of recipes inserted into narratives concerning the lives of a variety
of people, including a shepherd, a housewife in San Sebastián, a tuna fisherman from
Ondárroa, and a *kaiku*-maker (a maker of wooden milking pitchers), living in the
Spanish Basque region. The passages tend to be idealized and nostalgic, but are
representative of traditional life.

349 **The Spanish kitchen.**
Pepita Aris.   London: Cassell, 1998. 223p. map.
The revised edition of *The Spanishwoman's kitchen* (1992). The author gives first a
description of Spanish cuisine region by region, and then includes some one hundred
recipes arranged by type of dish. At the end of each descriptive chapter, references
guide the reader to the recipes corresponding to the particular region. The distinctive
qualities of Basque cookery (and all-male cooking societies, a long-established custom
of the region) are discussed on p. 59-66, and eleven recipes characteristic of the region
are included.

350 **Traditional Basque cooking, history and preparation.**
José María Busca Isusi.   Reno, Nevada; Las Vegas: University of
Nevada Press, 1987. 205p. bibliog. (The Basque Series).
A translation of the 1983 Spanish edition of this work by a leading Basque chef and
writer on cookery. It consists of six sections, the first of which is a survey of cooking
utensils, eating habits and methods of preparation, drawn from historical sources. The
next four sections are devoted to typical foods and methods of preparing them, covering
vegetables, meat and poultry, fish and seafood, eggs, deserts, dairy produce and
drinks. A selection of traditional recipes concludes the work. There is a full index with
terms in English and in Spanish, or Basque as appropriate.

Folklore, Festivals and Costume

351 **Alardeak.** (Military parades.)
Juan Antonio Urbeltz, photographs by Lamia. Donostia-San
Sebastián, Spain: Gipuzkoako Foru Aldundia, Kultura eta Turismo
Saila = Diputación Foral de Gipuzkoa, Departamento de Cultura y
Turismo, 1995. 120p. bibliog. (Bertan, no. 8).

This introductory study considers the symbolic significance of parades of soldiers and
women dressed as *cantinières*. These parades were held to mark the successful
defence of Gipuzkoa, the Feasts of St. Sebastian and St. John the Baptist, and Corpus
Christi. The most famous are held in Fuenterrabia in honour of the Virgin Mary, and
in Irún in honour of St. Martial. (These last parades have become a matter of dispute,
because of the desire of women to participate as soldiers). There are many photographs in black-and-white and in colour, and the English text appears at the end.

352 **Basque legends: collected, chiefly in the Labourd.**
Wentworth Webster. London: Griffith & Farran, 1877. 233p.

The Rev. Webster (1828-1907) was Anglican chaplain in St.-Jean-de-Luz and retired
subsequently to Sare. A keen student of Basque folklore, he collected and translated this
anthology of Basque legends. There is a short general introduction, and each tale or group
of tales is preceded by a brief analysis and comparison with similar legends in other
traditions. The book also includes an essay on the Basque language by Julien Vinson.

353 **Basque legends in their social context.**
Elena Arana Williams. In: *Essays in Basque social anthropology and
history.* Edited by William A. Douglass. Reno, Nevada: Basque
Studies Program, University of Nevada, 1989, p. 107-27. (Basque
Studies Program Occasional Paper Series, no. 4).

Illustrates how a number of Basque folktales concerning *lamiak* (supernatural female
figures) from the Barandiarán collection reinforce the contemporary social norms of
rural communities.

354   **Carnaval en Navarra.** (Carnival in Navarra.)
Juan Garmendia Larrañaga.   San Sebastián, Spain: Haranburu, 1984.
255p. (Ensayos de etnografía, no. 3).
A description of the various fiestas associated with Carnival in Navarra, arranged alphabetically by place.

355   **Diccionario de mitología vasca.** (Dictionary of Basque mythology.)
José Miguel de Barandiarán.   San Sebastián, Spain: Txertoa, 1984.
219p. (Ipar Haizea, no. 19).
Provides an essential introduction to Basque myth and legend. It embraces animal and half-human spirits, places (e.g. caves, woods), the elements, legends associated with particular locations, and beliefs (e.g. in chance). The entries for widespread beliefs, e.g. in *lamiak* and in *mari*, are extensive. Headwords are in Basque.

356   **Fiestas, costumbres y leyendas de Navarra.** (Fiestas, customs and
legends of Navarra.)
Luis Pedro Peña Santiago.   San Sebastian Spain: Txertoa, 1984. 102p.
(Askatasun Haizea, no. 70).
A short anthology of popular tales, legends and descriptions of particular fiestas, most notably Carnival, in Navarra.

357   **Korrika. Basque ritual for ethnic identity.**
Teresa del Valle.   Reno, Nevada; Las Vegas; London: University of
Nevada Press, 1994. 223p. bibliog. (The Basque Series).
A translation of *Korrika. Rituales de la lengua en el espacio*, an anthropological study of *korrika*, an annual event (beating the bounds) that since 1980 has involved thousands of people running to the four corners of the Basque Country. The race serves to generate popular support for the Basque language and seeks a re-affirmation of Basque identity and unity. Del Valle discusses the participants, stressing the role of women and children, and also analyses differences between political groupings in their support for *korrika*. Traditional symbols and activities are interpreted in terms of present-day Basque identity.

358   **Legends and popular tales of the Basque people.**
Mariana Monteiro, with illustrations in photogravure by Harold
Copping.   London: T. Fisher Unwin, 1887. 274p.
A less well-known anthology than Webster's (item no. 352), produced in a fine limited edition, and subsequently in a popular edition by the same publisher in 1890.

359   **Petit dictionnaire de mythologies basque et pyrénéenne.** (Concise
dictionary of Basque and Pyrenean mythology.)
Olivier de Marliave.   Paris: Editions Entente, 1993. 294p.
(Mythologies).
A useful dictionary for the general reader that includes the mythology of Catalans, Aragonese and Gascons, as well as Basques. The entries are fairly brief and include deities, giants, spirits, symbolic places and objects, personnages in folklore, popular religion and customs.

360   **Pyrenean festivals. Calendar customs, music & magic. Dance & drama.**
Violet Alford.   London: Chatto & Windus, 1937. 286p.
A vivid description (p. 135-200) of customs in both the Spanish and French regions, organized according to the festivals of the calendar year, and drawing on both historical sources and more recent eyewitness accounts. Music and dance are dealt with in the greatest detail, but more barbaric customs involving the death of birds and animals are also included. Comparisons are made with other European traditions.

361   **Los sanfermines.** (The fiesta of San Fermín.)
Photographs by Ramón Masats, text by Rafael García Serrano.
Madrid: Espasa-Calpe, 1963. 275p.
The publisher's own words rightly describe the book's text as a 'soundtrack', complementing the photographs of Masats. These latter, nearly all black-and-white, are vivid and evocative of the occasion. They, and the text, follow a twenty-four-hour period during the fiesta, from evening, through the night, to dawn and the running of the bulls (the famous 'encierro'), and on into the morning and afternoon. The book also records the eating and drinking, the processions, dancing, Basque sports and other traditional customs of the fiesta as it was in the 1960s and as it had been up until that time. Both photographer and writer instantly reveal their enthusiasm for the spectacle. A number of additional photographs are by Pamplona Cine-Foto and are graphic scenes of individuals or groups of runners caught by the bulls. (The text is in four languages – Spanish, French, English and German. Thus, the descriptions are shorter than the bibliographic details indicate.)

362   **Singing duels and social solidarity: the case of the Basque**
Charivari.
Roslyn M. Frank.   In: *Essays in Basque social anthropology and history.*   Edited by William A Douglass.   Reno, Nevada: Basque Studies Program, University of Nevada, 1989, p. 43-80. (Basque Studiesa Program Occasional Papers Series, no. 4).
An analysis of the Basque *charivari*, or mock trial, in which a real-life violation of a social norm was re-enacted by villagers and its protagonists judged. Frank studies in depth the trial in *ca.* 1815, recorded by Wentworth Webster in the Pays Basque, of an elderly man about to wed for a fourth time, and whose three previous wives had died in childbirth. She links features of the *charivari* to other contemporaneous folk customs, and discusses the role of the *bertsolari* (oral poet) in the trials, and its relation to debates between modern *bertsolariak*.

363   **Tradiciones y costumbres del País Vasco.** (Traditions and customs of the Basque Country.)
Alfredo Feliú Corcuera.   San Sebastián, Spain: Kriselu, 1987. 4 vols.
(Gure Herria).
A descriptive account of popular festivals, mostly in the Spanish region. The work follows the calendar year, illustrating the most memorable and important festivals in particular places. A preliminary summary outlines the central subject of the festival (*tema*), describes its activities and lists where it takes place.

364 **Vascos y trajes.** (Basques and costumes.)
María Elena de Arizmendi Amiel.   San Sebastián, Spain: Caja de
Ahorros Muncipial de San Sebastián, 1976. 2 vols.

Chronological description of traditional clothes and military uniforms worn by
Basques, from both the Spanish and French regions and Navarra. The study is based
upon contemporary illustrations and, where these are lacking, on reconstructions
based on written descriptions and hypotheses. There are many reproductions,
augmented by photographs and drawings. Also included are descriptions of modern
festivals, and of the *pastorales* of Soule.

365 **A view from the witch's cave. Folktales of the Pyrenees.**
Edited by Luis de Barandiarán Irizar, collected with a prologue by José
Miguel de Barandiarán, foreword by Joseba Zulaika, translated by
Linda White.   Reno, Nevada; Las Vegas: University of Nevada Press,
1991. 131p. (The Basque Series).

A translation of *Breve antología de fábulas, cuentos y leyendas del País Vasco* (San
Sebastián, Spain: Txertoa, 1988). This is an anthology of fourteen fables, twenty-one
folk tales and twenty-nine legends from the collection of a pioneering Basque folklorist. The animal fables are in the Aesopic tradition, while the folk tales have Basque
settings but are variations on universal themes, including Cinderella, Tom Thumb, etc.
The legends are brief and deal with other-worldly figures, notably *lamiak*, Basque
sorceresses or sirens.

Sports and Recreation

366 **El gran libro de la pelota: deporte universal.** (The book of pelota: the universal sport.)
Luis Bombín Fernández, Rodolfo Bozas-Urrutia.   Madrid: Tipografía Artística, 1976. 2 vols. bibliog.

Covers all aspects of the sport known in Basque as *jai alai* and elsewhere as pelota. The authors examine the history of the game in the Basque region and elsewhere, including the United States, and discuss organizations concerned with pelota in Spain. There are also chapters on famous pelota players and on the terminology of the sport. Bombín Fernández was also author of the earlier *Historia, ciencia y código de pelota* (Barcelona: Lauro, 1946).

367 **Grands sportifs du Pays Basque.** (Great sportsmen of the Basque Country.)
Eskutik [i.e. Louis Toulet].   Donostia, Spain; Bayonne, France: Elkar, 1990. 205p.

A series of interviews with eighteen famous, retired French Basque sports players (seventeen men and one woman), arranged by sport: tennis (Jean Borotra), cycling, boxing, rowing, rugby and pelota.

368 **Nosotros los vascos: juegos y deportes.** (We Basques: sports and games.)
Donostia, Spain: Lur, 1990. 5 vols.

A comprehensive and lavishly illustrated work devoted both to truly indigenous sports, and to those from outside adopted and adapted by the Basques. Sporting activity is set in its socio-historical context. The five volumes cover pelota, log-chopping, weightlifting, rowing, running, rural sports, sport for women, mountaineering and rock-climbing.

Libraries, Art Galleries, Museums and Archives

369 **Censo de bibliotecas del País Vasco.** (Census of libraries of the Basque Country.)
Edited by Ander Manterola Aldecoa.   San Sebastián, Spain: Eusko Ikaskuntza, 1989. 3 vols. bibliog.

A comprehensive guide to all libraries in the Basque Autonomous Community, with one volume for each province, arranged by type of library (public, professional, religious, museum etc.). The information includes the type of catalogue available, nature and extent of stock, services and state of preservation of stock. There are also detailed statistical tables.

370 **Museo de Navarra.** (Museum of Navarra.)
Pamplona, Spain: Gobierno de Navarra, Departamento de Educación y Cultura, 1989. 224p.

An attractively illustrated guide to the history and holdings of the provincial museum in Pamplona. The museum focuses on the periods shared with the rest of the Iberian Peninsula – Roman, Visigothic, Hispano-Arabic, and Romanesque – rather than on indigenous Basque culture. Particularly noteworthy are the 14th century mural paintings transferred from Pamplona cathedral. The museum also holds a collection of Navarrese painting, and some pieces of sculpture by Jorge Oteiza (from Orio, Gipuzkoa).

371 **Museoak Euskadi = Euskadi museos.** (Basque museums.)
Vitoria-Gasteiz, Spain: Gobierno Vasco, Departamento de Cultura = Eusko Jaurlaritza, Kultura Saila, 1995. 172p.

A guide to the major museums and art galleries of the Basque Autonomous Community. Each entry gives practical information (address, telephone number, opening hours, etc.), followed by a history of the institution and a description of the collections. The text is in Basque with a parallel Spanish translation.

Catálogo de publicaciones periódicas vascas de los siglos XIX-XX.
See item no. 376.

The Book Trade

372 **Artes gráficas. Una introducción a la historia de la imprenta en el País Vasco.** (Graphic art. Introduction to the history of printing in the Basque Country.)
Iban Zaldua, Pilar Mur, Xabier Madariaga.   Bilbao, Spain: Bizkaiko Foru Aldundia = Diputación Foral de Bizkaia, 1995. 115p. bibliog.

A collection of five essays in Spanish on various topics relating to book production in Bizkaia and in the Basque Region in general: the history of the paper-making industry in Bizkaia; engraving and book illustration in Bizkaia; printing and engraving in Bizkaia; the origins of lithography in the Basque Region; and the history of book binding in the Basque Region.

373 **Le livre et l'imprimerie dans les Pyrénées françaises.** (The book and printing in the French Pyrenees.)
Lourdes, France: Musée Pyrénéen, 1976. 222p. bibliog.

A catalogue of an exhibition held at the Musée Pyrénéen, Château Fort de Lourdes (June – October 1976). The introduction includes a brief essay on books and reading in Béarn and the Pays Basques in the post-medieval period (by C. Desplat), and essays on printing in the regions bordering the Pays Basque. The catalogue proper is organized by place of printing, and includes works printed in Bayonne and St.-Jean-de-Luz. There are black-and-white photographs of selected title-pages.

XX. Mendeko euskal liburuen katalogoa (1900-1992).
See item no. 399.

XXXII. Euskal liburu eta disko azoka.
See item no. 400.

Essai d'une bibliographie de la langue basque.
See item no. 406.

Mass Media

374 **Los medios de comunicación en Euskadi.** (The media in Euskadi.)
Edited by Ramón Zallo, Alberto Díaz Mancisidor. Leoia, Spain:
Universidad del País Vasco, 1990. 149p. (Cuadernos de Extensión
Universitaria, no. 36).

A collection of short introductory essays, intended for university students, but also of
wider interest. It covers press, television, radio and publishing, and also includes a
cultural profile of the Spanish Basque region and of the media in nations which are not
states.

375 **Los medios de comunicación en el País Vasco.** (The media in the
Basque Country.)
Co-ordinated by César Coca, Florencio Martínez. Bilbao [?], Spain:
Universidad del País Vasco, 1993. 136p. bibliog. (Amerika eta
euskaldunak = América y los vascos).

A most useful survey of the press, radio and television in the Basque Autonomous
Community, focusing largely upon the post-Franco period. The first chapter charts the
changes in the daily press during and after the transition to democracy, and the emergence of new titles. The second consists of a brief history of the daily newspapers,
indicating their political affiliations (if any) and editorial policy. The third and fourth
chapters are very brief overviews of magazine publishing and of radio and television.
Statistics regarding print runs, readership and audience figures are included in an
appendix.

The Press

General

376 **Catálogo de publicaciones periódicas vascas de los siglos XIX-XX.**
(Catalogue of Basque periodical publications of the 19th-20th
centuries.)
Adolfo Ruiz de Gauna.   San Sebastián, Spain: Eusko Ikaskuntza;
Vitoria-Gasteiz, Spain: Eusko Jaurlaritza, Kultura eta Turismo Saila =
Gobierno Vasco, Departamento de Cultura y Turismo, 1991. 710p.
bibliog.

Lists by title periodical publications (including newspapers) published in the Basque
Region, or of Basque interest published elsewhere, and gives details of place and date
of publication, publisher, frequency, language and the holdings of libraries in the
region and in the rest of the world. Also included is a listing of those libraries,
together with addresses and telephone numbers, a chronological index of periodicals
by starting date, a geographical index by place of publication, a subject index, a
politico-ideological index, and an index by holding library. The work ends with various tables of publication statistics.

Newspapers

In addition to the titles listed below, the national dailies *El mundo,* since May 1991, and *El País,* since May 1997, have both produced editions for the Basque region. The title of the former is *El mundo del siglo veintiuno del País Vasco.*

377 **El correo español – El pueblo vasco.** (The Spanish post – the Basque people.)
Bilbao, Spain: Bilbao Editorial, 1938- . daily.

An independent daily newspaper in Spanish, formed by the merger in 1938 of *El correo español* (established 1937) and *El pueblo vasco* (established 1901). There has been an edition in Alava since 1946.

378 **Deia: gure lurraren deia.** (The crier: the crier of our country.)
Bilbao, Spain: Iparaguirre, 1977- . daily.

A nationalist daily newspaper, in Basque and Spanish, which supports the political line of the Basque Nationalist Party. Since February 1978, there have been separate editions for each Spanish Basque province and for Navarra.

379 **Diario de Navarra.** (Navarra daily.)
Pamplona, Spain: Diario de Navarra, S.A., 1903- . daily.

A conservative daily newspaper in Spanish, produced in Navarra, but available and read elsewhere in the Spanish Basque region.

380 **Diario de noticias.** (Daily news.)
Pamplona, Spain: Zeroa Multimedia, 1994- . daily.

A Navarrese daily newspaper in Spanish – the continuation of *Navarra hoy* (Navarra today).

381 **El diario vasco.** (Basque daily.)
San Sebastián, Spain: Sociedad Vascongada de Publicaciones, 1934- . daily.

An independent, non-nationalist daily newspaper in Spanish.

382 **Egin.** (Action.)
Hernani, Spain: Orain, 1977- . daily.

A militantly nationalistic daily newspaper in Basque and Spanish. Its political ideology is close to that of Herri Batasuna, considered to be the political wing of ETA. The newspaper's closure was ordered by law on 15 July 1998 on account of its connections with ETA.

383 **Euskaldun egunkaria.** (Basque newspaper.)
Donostia, Spain: Egunkaria Elkarte Anonimoa, 1990- . daily.

A nationalist, left-leaning, newspaper in Basque that was first published on 15 July 1990.

384   **El periódico de Álava = Arabako egunkaria.** (Alava daily news.)
      Vitoria-Gasteiz, Spain: El Periódico de Alava, S.A., 1996- . daily.
A daily newspaper in Basque which is culturally pro-Basque, but not especially
nationalistic.

385   **La Semaine du Pays Basque.** (Pays Basque weekly press.)
      Bayonne, France: Les Éditions de la Semaine, 1993- . weekly.
A weekly local newspaper for the French Basque region, in French.

386   **Sud Ouest. Grand quotidien republicain régional d'information.**
      Pays Basque. (South West. Regional Republican daily newspaper.
      Pays Basque.)
      Bordeaux, France: [Sept.] 1944- . daily.
A non-nationalist daily newspaper in French.

Magazines

387   **Emakunde.** (Woman.)
      Vitoria-Gasteiz, Spain: Instituto Vasco de la Mujer, 1989- . quarterly.
A quarterly magazine devoted to women's issues and issues from a woman's perspective.
The articles are in Basque or Spanish, and do not focus exclusively on the Basque
region.

388   **Euskadi.**
      Hernani, Spain: Orain, 1982[?]- . annual.
Now published annually by the militant nationalist daily, *Egin*, this illustrated review
of the past year in the Basque region began with an issue covering 1977-82. Together
with the important events of each year, it covers economics, politics, sport, culture and
language issues. It is written in Basque or Spanish.

389   **Pays Basque magazine.**
      Toulouse, France: Milan Presse and Editions de la Semaine, 1996- .
      quarterly.
A quarterly illustrated magazine in French devoted to the culture, geography, history
and cuisine of the Basque Region (both French and Spanish).

Periodicals

390   Basque Artistic Expression.
Indiana, Pennsylvania: Society of Basque Studies, 1980-81.
One of the very few journals devoted to Basque culture, especially to literature, that published articles in English. It was superseded by item no. 392.

391   Basque Studies Program Newsletter.
Reno, Nevada: University of Nevada, 1968- . biannual.
A twice-yearly newsletter, which includes information about research on Basque-related subjects carried out by the staff, graduate students and visiting researchers at the University of Nevada. It also has information on the library holdings concerning Basque studies, which are excellent.

392   Journal of Basque Studies.
Indiana, Pennsylvania: Society of Basque Studies in America, 1982-84.
Continues item no. 390. The articles published cover a wide range of topics relating to both the French and Spanish regions: literature, language, history, anthropology, art and folklore. These are largely in English, but some are in Spanish. After vol. 5, no. 1, the Society of Basque Studies in America split into two bodies. One retained the name, the other became the Basque American Foundation. The latter continued publishing the *Journal of Basque Studies* until 1993. (The Foundation itself has been defunct since 1995.) The former publishes the *Journal of Basque Studies in America* (subsequently *Journal of the Society of Basque Studies in America* from vol. 8, 1988). It is now published at Fresno State University, Fresno, California.

393   Príncipe de Viana.
Pamplona, Spain: Diputación Foral de Navarra, 1940- . quarterly.
A major quarterly journal publishing scholarly articles mainly on the arts, history, language, politics and religion of Navarra. It is edited at the research institute known as the Institución Príncipe de Viana, and is now published by the Departamento de Educación y Cultura of the Gobierno de Navarra.

394 **Revue Internationale des Études Basques.** (International Journal of
Basque Studies.)
Paris, 1907-36.
An extremely important periodical publishing articles in French or in Spanish, mostly
on Basque language and literature, but also on other aspects of Basque culture.

Catálogo de publicaciones periódicas vascas de los siglos XIX-XX.
See item no. 376.

Encyclopaedias and Directories

395 **Diccionario enciclopédico del País Vasco.** (Encyclopedic dictionary of the Basque Country.)
San Sebastián, Spain: Haranburu, 1985. 10 vols.

A basic, alphabetical encyclopedia of both the French and Spanish Basque regions, which is less ambitious than Auñamendi (item no. 396). It covers both humanities and social sciences, but is strongest on history, geography, ethnography and biography. It is well illustrated, but the bibliography is limited.

396 **Enciclopedia general ilustrada del País Vasco.** (General illustrated encyclopedia of the Basque Country.)
San Sebastián, Spain: Auñamendi, Estornés Lasa, 1970- . maps.

A colossal work of enormous reference value, but which is still incomplete and inevitably becoming out-dated. It is divided into three parts (*cuerpos*): A (*Diccionario enciclopédico vasco*), an encyclopedia arranged alphabetically; B (*Enciclopedia sistemática*), an encyclopedia arranged by subject; and C, a bibliography (see item no. 407). *Cuerpo* A covers the entire Basque region, its history, culture, sport, literature, family names and achievements of persons of Basque origin all over the world (e.g. Simón Bolívar). There are bibliographies at the end of each article. Forty-five volumes (to *Super*-) had appeared by 1997. *Cuerpo* B consists so far of three parts. A five-volume history of literature contains biographies of authors, histories of individual movements and, a most useful feature, selected passages in Spanish translation. The *Historia general de Euskalerria* (General history of the Basque Country) has so far advanced as far as the period of the kingdom of Pamplona and the death of Sancho VII in 1234. The first volume covers prehistory, and subsequent volumes comprise a traditional chronological history of the whole of the region, with chapters on social and cultural history, beliefs and religion, and the law. One volume only has appeared of *Etnología y sociología de los vascos* (Ethnology and sociology of the Basques), dealing with the family and social organization. In addition, there is a separate volume, entitled *Juegos y deportes vascos* (Basque games and sports), by Rafael Aguirre Franco.

397   **Gran enciclopedia Navarra.** (The encyclopedia of Navarre.)
Pamplona, Spain: Caja de Ahorros de Navarra, 1990. 11 vols.
A general, illustrated encyclopaedia, arranged alphabetically, which is strong on the history and geography of towns and cities, and persons of Navarrese origin. There is a limited bibliography under major entries.

398   **Komunikazioaren gidaliburua = Guía de la comunicación: Euskadi 1996.** (Information guide: Euskadi 1996.)
Gobierno Vasco, Dirección de Prensa y Comunicación. [Vitoria-Gasteiz, Spain]: Eusko Jaurlaritza, Lehendakaritza = Gobierno Vasco, Presidencia del Gobierno, 1995. 494p.
The latest edition of a comprehensive directory covering the Basque Government and Parliament (principal appointments and representatives), public companies, provincial administrations, the church, education, political parties, trade unions and business organizations, chambers of commerce, and the media.

Bibliographies

399 **XX. Mendeko euskal liburuen katalogoa (1900-1992).** (Catalogue of Basque books of the 20th century.)
Joan Mari Torreldai Nabea.   Donostia, Spain: Gipuzkoako Foru Aldundia, Kultura eta Turismo Departamentua, 1993. 1,187p.
A catalogue of books in Basque arranged by subject according to the UNESCO classification system, plus indexes by author (personal and corporate) and by title. Two supplements have been published: 1993-94 (1995, 240p.) and 1995-96 (1997, 251p.). The introduction to each volume analyses trends in Basque book production.

400 **XXXII. Euskal liburu eta disko azoka.** (Catalogue of the XXXII Basque Book and Record Fair.)
Bilbao, Spain: Gerediaga Elkartea and Bilbao Bizkaia Kutxa, 1997. 955p.
The Basque Book (and Record) Fair has been held in Durango (Bizkaia) since 1965. The catalogue, which has appeared nearly every year, is a most valuable reference tool, arranged by publisher with indexes by title and author. It functions as a 'Basque books in print'.

401 **Autores vascos.** (Basque writers.)
Elías Amézaga.   Bilbao, Spain: Gorka, 1984-87. 10 vols.
Lists alphabetically authors and writers of Basque origin, but cites only their works in Spanish. Writers on the sciences as well as the humanities are covered. Amézaga gives brief biographical details of each writer at the head of each entry. At the start of each volume there is a bibliography of the authors contained in that volume.

402 **Basque Americans: a guide to information sources.**
William A. Douglass, Richard W. Etulain. Detroit, Michigan: Gale
Research Company, 1981. 169p. (Ethnic Studies Information Guide
Series, vol. 6).

A critical bibliography containing 413 entries arranged by subject and comprising not
only books and articles, but also films, documentaries, recorded music and libraries in
the United States that have important Basque holdings. Although the work focuses on
the history of Basques in the United States, several sections contain useful items about
the European Basque Region, including bibliographies and reference works, periodicals, physical anthropology, language, folklore, sports, games and festivals, and art
and music. Directly concerned with Basque Americans are the chapters on the social
sciences, literature, education, cookbooks and hotels.

403 **Bibliographie de la langue basque (Complément & supplément).
Critique.** (Bibliography of Basque [Complement and supplement].
Critique.)
Edward Spencer Dodgson. Dax, France: Imprimerie-Reliure H.
Labèque, 1899. 11p.

A series of corrections to the translations of titles contained in the second part of
Vinson's *Essai* (item no. 406).

404 **Catálogo de obras euskaras, o, Catálogo general cronológico de las
obras impresas referentes á las provincias de Álava, Guipúzcoa,
Bizcaya, Navarra, etc.** (Catalogue of Basque works, or, General
chronological catalogue of printed books referring to the provinces of
Alava, Gipuzkoa, Bizkaia, Navarra, etc.)
Genaro de Sorarrain. Barcelona, Spain, 1891. 492p. Reprinted,
Bilbao, Spain: Caja de Ahorros Vizcaina, 1984. 500p. (Colección
Bibliográfica. Serie Mayor, no. 3).

A catalogue of both books in Basque, and of books about the Spanish Basque region
in other languages (largely Spanish and French), with the author's comments. It is still
of use.

405 **Catalogue des manuscrits celtiques et basques de la Bibliothéque
Nationale.** (Catalogue of Celtic and Basque manuscripts in the
Bibliothèque Nationale.)
Henri Omont. Paris, 1890. 46p. (Extract from *Revue Celtique*, no. 11,
p. 389-432).

Lists three 17th-century manuscripts. in the hand of Silvain Pouvreau, a priest in the
diocese of Bourges. One contains his Basque-French dictionary, the second the same
dictionary, plus miscellaneous items relating to the Basque language, and the third his
Basque version of the *Imitatio Christi*.

406   **Essai d'une bibliographie de la langue basque.** (Towards a Basque bibliography.)
Julien Vinson.   Paris, 1891, 1898. 2 vols. Reprinted, Bilbao, Spain: Caja de Ahorros Vizcaina, 1983. (Colección Bibliográfica. Serie Mayor, no. 1).

A work of immeasurable value that gives a bibliographical description of virtually every book printed in Basque from 1545 to the 1890s. The arrangement is chronological, although subsequent editions are placed immediately after the first edition of a work. It is indexed by author (or translator), place of printing and subject. The bibliographical transcription (title, imprint, etc.) of each work is translated into French at the foot of the appropriate page. A supplement and a list of proposed corrections were published by Edward Spencer Dodgson in 1892 and 1899 (items nos. 403 and 410).

407   **Eusko Bibliographia.** (Basque bibliography.)
Jon Bilbao.   San Sebastián, Spain: Auñamendi; Estornés Lasa, 1970-81. 10 vols.

This invaluable work corresponds to Cuerpo C of the monumental *Enciclopedia general ilustrada del País Vasco* (item no. 396). It includes books, pamphlets and periodical articles, mostly in Spanish, French or Basque (although some are in English) on the Basque region from the beginning of printing until 1975, arranged under author, subject and place-names. The extent of items is also given, which permits identification of editions of frequently published works. The contents lists of periodicals, which appear within the alphabetical sequence (under title of the periodical), are also very useful.

408   **Eusko-Bibliographia 1976-1980.** (Basque bibliography 1976-80.)
Jon Bilbao.   Bilbao, Spain: Universidad del País Vasco, 1985-87. 3 vols.

Continues item no. 407 above. A further supplement to 1961-75 is included in vol. 3.

409   **Eusko-Bibliographia 1981-1985.** (Basque bibliography 1981-85.)
Jon Bilbao.   Bilbao, Spain: Universidad del País Vasco, 1996- .

Continues items nos. 407 and 408 above. So far only vol. 1 (A-B) has appeared. With Bilbao's death in 1994 it is uncertain whether the work will be completed.

410   **Supplément à la Bibliographie de la langue basque.** (Supplement to the Basque bibliography.)
Edward Spencer Dodgson.   Paris: Émile Bouillon, 1892. 2 parts. (Extract from *Revue des bibliothèques,* no. 2 [1892], p. 216-27, p. 529-47).

Adds items omitted from Vinson's *Essai* (no. 406), or items which appeared after the publication of the first part.

Indexes

There follow three separate indexes: authors (personal or corporate); titles; and subjects. Title entries are italicized and refer either to the main titles, or to other works cited in the annotations. The numbers refer to bibliographical entry rather than page number. Individual index entries are arranged in alphabetical sequence.

Index of Authors

S

Sáez García, Juan Antonio 34
Saizarbitoria, Ramón 295, 300, 307
Saltarelli, Mario 145
San Martín, Juan 7
Santana, Alberto 186
Santoyo, Julio-César 99
Sarasola, Ibon 167, 291
Schommer, Alberto 25
Scott, J. M. 30
Sebeok, Thomas A. 144
Segurola Jiménez, Marco 34
Sesmero Pérez, Francisco 60
Sevilla, María José 348
Shafir, Gershon 217
Shelley, Ronald G. 99
Sim, Richard 198
Smith, Christine 51, 53
Smith, Trevor C. 65
Sneath, Guy 54
Society of Basque Studies 390
Society of Basque Studies in America 392
Sorarrain, Genaro de 404
Sota, Manuel de la 168
Southworth, Herbert Rutledge 110
Spanish Philatelic Society 99
Starkie, Walter 31
Steer, G. L. 118
Stephens, Meic 196, 199
Stevenson, John 150
Sturrock, John 17
Suárez Fernández, Luis 26
Suhubiette, Jean 233
Sullivan, John 212

T

Tasende, J. M. 319
Tellagorri, Mikel 49
Thomas, Gordon 103
Thomas, Henk 252
Thomas, Ned 196
Thompson, Charles William 99, 119
Tone, John Lawrence 105
Torreldai Nabea, Joan Mari 399
Toulet, Louis see Eskutik
Tovar, Antonio 141, 146, 166
Trask, R. L. 142, 156, 162
Tuduri, José Luis 345
Txillardegi 295, 299

U

Unsain, José María 343
Unwin, Tim 4
Urbeltz, Juan Antonio 351
Urla, Jacqueline 193
Urretabizkaia, Arantxa 295, 309, 312

V

Valle, Teresa del 357
Veyrin, Philippe 11, 14, 21

Veyriras, Paul 332
Victoria and Albert Museum (London) 327
Viers, Georges 7, 38
Villasante, Luis 290
Vinson, Julien 352, 403, 406, 410

W

Walton, John K. 24
Webster, Wentworth 352
Wheeler, Robert 268
White, Linda 164, 169, 365
Wilbur, Terence H. 142, 159
Wilson, Arnold 108
Wingrave, Helen 340
Wolfram, Herwig 73
Woodman, Francis 57
II World Basque Congress see II Euskal Mundu Biltzarra

Y

Ysursa, John M. 335

Z

Zaldua, Iban 372
Zallo, Ramón 374
Zirakzadeh, Cyrus Ernesto 195, 220
Zulaika, Joseba 187, 195, 365

Index of Titles

133

Index of Subjects

144

Industrialization
  French region 231
  Gipuzkoa 261, 264
Iron industry
  Bilbao 241-42
Iron mining industry
  Bizkaia 271

J

Jews
  Navarre (Kingdom)
  82-83, 85

K

Korrika 357

L

Labour movement
  Bizkaia 271
Labourd
  Catholic Church 180
  maps 44
  witchcraft 180
Lancre, Pierre de 180
Language, Basque 3-4,
    6-7, 13-14, 25, 72, 74,
    87, 141, 146, 160,
    388, 392
  bibliographies 150
  courses 171-72
  dialects 146, 157
  dictionaries 163-70
  etymology 143, 151-52,
    161
  French region 147,
    232
  grammar 142, 144-46,
    153-59, 162
  history 153, 156, 162
  ikastolak 209
  law 222, 224
  manuscripts 405
  Navarra 393
  origins 146, 149, 156
  phonology 145, 148,
    153, 157, 162
  repression 199, 208

social aspects 122,
    124, 126, 147, 153,
    232
  Spanish region 183,
    209, 222-24
  teaching 153, 209, 280,
    391
  use in liturgy 175
  vocabulary 156
Law 396
  anti-terrorism 228
  Basque Autonomous
    Community 222-25,
    227
  French region 184
  language 222, 224
  nationality 224
  Navarra 226
  Spain 228
  taxation 223
Legends 352, 358, 365
  dictionaries 355,
    359
Liberalism
  Spanish region 176,
    178
Libraries 376
  Basque Autonomous
    Community 369
  directories 369
Literature, Basque 6-7, 26,
    87, 146
  bertsolaritza 2, 10, 14,
    21, 187, 285-86, 292
  drama 5-6, 15, 21
  fiction 295
  history and criticism
    283-84, 287, 289-91,
    293, 388, 390, 392,
    396
  pastorales 6
  poetry 2, 10, 14, 21,
    285, 294, 296, 304,
    310
  translations 295-313
  women writers 288
Liturgy
  Catholic Church 175
Local government
  Basque Autonomous
    Community 23
  French region 21,
    233

M

Magazines
  catalogues 376
  French region 389
  Spanish region
    387-88
Mañeru (Navarra) 176
Manor houses
  Gipuzkoa 331
Manuscripts 405
  catalogues 405
Maps
  Alava 46
  Basse Navarre 43
  Bizkaia 46
  Côte d'argent 42
  Gipuzkoa 46
  Labourd 42, 44
  Navarra 47
  Pyrenean region 45
  Soule 43
Media
  Basque Autonomous
    Community 374-75
Metalwork 327
Military uniforms 364
Minerals 41
Mondragón (Gipuzkoa)
  co-operatives 245, 249,
    251-53, 256-57
Mountaineering 39
Mountains 39
Museo de Bellas Artes
  (Bilbao) 326
Museo de Navarra
  (Pamplona) 370
Museums
  Basque Autonomous
    Community 371
  directories 371
Music 6-7, 10, 21, 336,
    339, 360
Mythology
  dictionaries 355, 359

N

Nationalism 4, 195-96,
    199
  French region 201
  Navarra 202

Map of the Basque Region

This map shows the more important features.

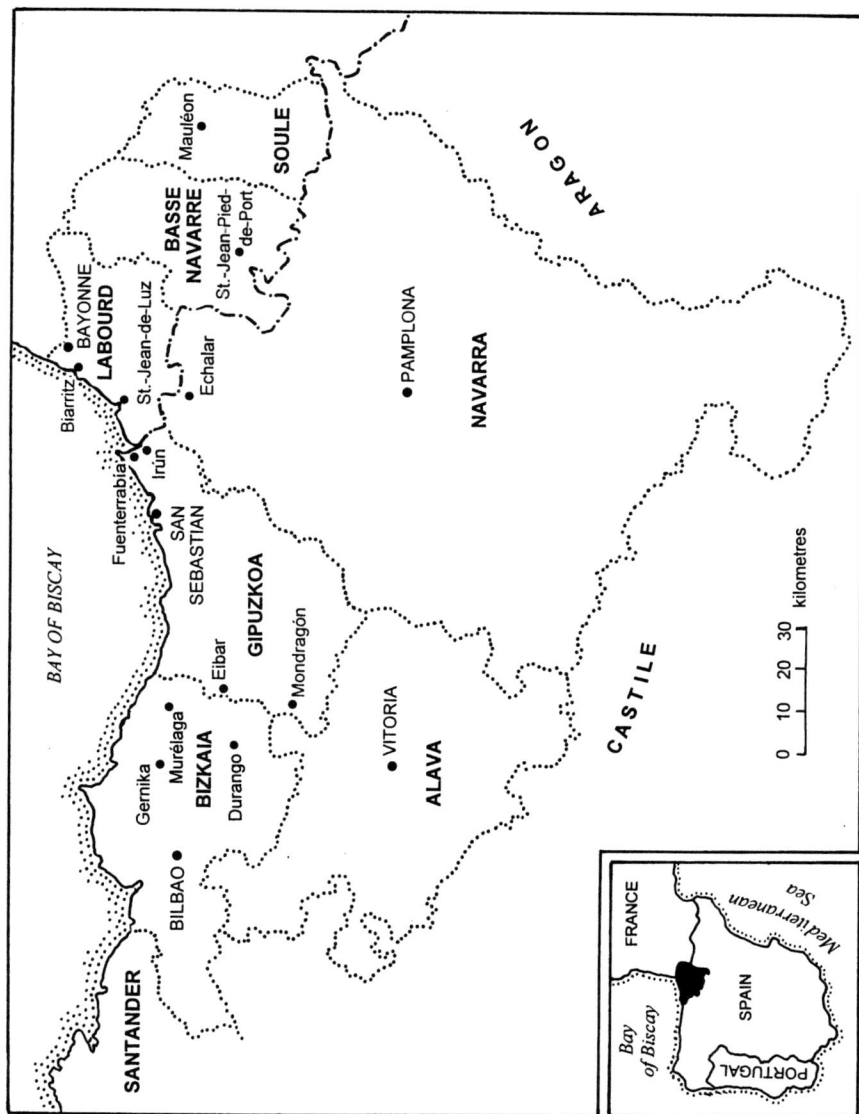

ALSO FROM CLIO PRESS

INTERNATIONAL ORGANIZATIONS SERIES

Each volume in the International Organizations Series is either devoted to one specific organization, or to a number of different organizations operating in a particular region, or engaged in a specific field of activity. The scope of the series is wide-ranging and includes intergovernmental organizations, international non-governmental organizations, and national bodies dealing with international issues. The series is aimed mainly at the English-speaker and each volume provides a selective, annotated, critical bibliography of the organization, or organizations, concerned. The bibliographies cover books, articles, pamphlets, directories, databases and theses and, wherever possible, attention is focused on material about the organizations rather than on the organizations' own publications. Notwithstanding this, the most important official publications, and guides to those publications, will be included. The views expressed in individual volumes, however, are not necessarily those of the publishers.

VOLUMES IN THE SERIES